Hands-On Artificial Intelligence for Banking

A practical guide to building intelligent financial applications using machine learning techniques

Jeffrey Ng, CFA
Subhash Shah

BIRMINGHAM - MUMBAI

Hands-On Artificial Intelligence for Banking

Commissioning Editor: Pravin Dhandre
Acquisition Editor: Nelson Morris
Content Development Editor: Athikho Sapuni Rishana
Senior Editor: Roshan Kumar
Technical Editor: Manikandan Kurup
Copy Editor: Safis Editing
Project Coordinator: Aishwarya Mohan
Proofreader: Safis Editing
Indexer: Priyanka Dhadke
Production Designer: Alishon Mendonca

First published: July 2020

Production reference: 1090720

Published by Packt Publishing Ltd.
Livery Place
35 Livery Street
Birmingham
B3 2PB, UK.

ISBN 978-1-78883-078-2

www.packt.com

Contributors

About the authors

Jeffrey Ng, CFA, works at Ping An OneConnect Bank (Hong Kong) Limited as Head of FinTech Solutions. His mandate is to advance the use of AI in banking and financial ecosystems. Prior to this, he headed up the data lab of BNP Paribas Asia Pacific, which constructed an AI and data analytics solution for business, and was the vice-chair of the French Chamber of Commerce's FinTech Committee in Hong Kong. In 2010, as one of the pioneers in applying client analytics to investment banking, he built the analytics team for the bank. He has undertaken AI projects in retail and commercial banks with PwC Consulting and GE Money. He graduated from Hong Kong Polytechnic University in computing and management and holds an MBA in finance from the Chinese University of Hong Kong.

> *I want to thank my family and university lecturers for their encouragement during the darkest point of my life (literally and emotionally). Thank God I have you all.*

Subhash Shah works as Head of Technology at AIMDek Technologies Pvt. Ltd. He is an experienced solutions architect with over 12 years' experience. He holds a degree in information technology. He is an advocate of open source development and its utilization in solving critical business problems at a reduced cost. His interests include microservices, data analysis, machine learning, AI, and databases. He is an admirer of quality code and **Test-Driven Development** (TDD). His technical skills include, but are by no means limited to, translating business requirements into scalable architecture, designing sustainable solutions, and project delivery. He is a coauthor of *MySQL 8 Administrator's Guide* and *Hands-On High Performance with Spring 5*.

About the reviewers

Anil Omanwar has a dynamic personality with a great passion for the latest technology trends and research. He has over 13 years of experience in researching cognitive computing, while NLP, machine learning, information visualization, and text analytics are just a few of his areas of research interest. He is proficient in sentiment analysis, questionnaire-based feedback, text clustering, and phrase extraction in diverse domains such as banking, oil and gas, life sciences, manufacturing, and retail. He currently works for IBM Australia as a data science platform specialist, developing and delivering cognitive, AI-enabled platforms and solutions for businesses. He holds multiple patents on emerging technologies, including NLP automation and device intelligence.

Thanks to my mentors, parents, and family for their guidance and support.

Pouya Jamshidiat is an award-winning product leader and strategist in AI, fintech, and life sciences. He is a featured speaker at Product School and co-author of *The AI Book*. He is the founder of Pioneer Minds Ltd. Previously, he worked with the Lloyds Banking Group as a senior product owner on the application of AI in various sectors of the bank. He introduced the most advanced search and knowledge management technologies to the Lloyds Banking Group. He has worked for IBM as a senior product design consultant and as a senior product owner at Monitise. He has designed mobile banking and commerce value propositions. Recently, Pouya made the move to the life sciences sector, joining Eagle Genomics to help them apply AI to solve the big challenges facing scientists.

Packt is searching for authors like you

If you're interested in becoming an author for Packt, please visit `authors.packtpub.com` and apply today. We have worked with thousands of developers and tech professionals, just like you, to help them share their insight with the global tech community. You can make a general application, apply for a specific hot topic that we are recruiting an author for, or submit your own idea.

Table of Contents

Preface

Remodeling your outlook on banking begins with keeping up to date with the latest and most effective approaches, such as **Artificial Intelligence (AI)**. *Hands-On Artificial Intelligence for Banking* is a practical guide that will help you advance in your career in the banking domain. The book will demonstrate AI implementations to make your banking services smoother, more cost-efficient, and accessible to clients, focusing on both the client- and server-side uses of AI.

You'll begin by learning about the importance of AI, while also gaining insights into the recent AI revolution in the banking industry. Next, you'll get hands-on machine learning experience, exploring how to use time series analysis and reinforcement learning to automate client procurements and banking and finance decisions. After this, you'll progress to learning about mechanizing capital market decisions, using automated portfolio management systems, and predicting the future of investment banking. In addition to this, you'll explore concepts such as building personal wealth advisors and the mass customization of client lifetime wealth. Finally, you'll get to grips with some real-world AI considerations in the field of banking.

By the end of this book, you'll be equipped with the skills you need to navigate the finance domain by leveraging the power of AI.

Who this book is for

- **Students** in banking or technologies are the target audience for the book as there is a vacuum in the publication space regarding how AI technologies are used in the banking and finance industry. This book aims to give a reasonably useful list of use cases commonly known in the public domain and provide real sample code that is easy to implement. With this book, I am trying to expound important use cases but not to give you a machine learning model that you can put in use the next day.

- For **bankers** who are already in the field, I'm sure this book will help you build your services in the long run. It may encourage you to challenge anything that is obviously different from the way a start-up would function if you were ever to start one. Changes need to be made inside-out and outside-in. For IT managers within banks, this will give you a concrete code base on how the technologies can be applied and which open source libraries are available. Perhaps you are not convinced about developing everything in-house for production purposes. This book serves as a code base for any experiments you wish to launch.

- For **investors**, aspiring start-up founders, or MBA students, this is the industry participant's effort to share our problems and challenges with you. Please make banking better by creating better products that fit our needs. I hope your investment journey is smooth.

- For **FinTech start-ups** who have started businesses in this field, this book provides you with the floor and encourages you to open source and collaborate on industry-wide challenges, rather than close sourcing your work.

- For **regulators**, this serves as a guide on what is happening in banking. Your job is instrumental in the adoption of AI in banking—while at the same time, you could challenge models and decisions and encourage research by opening up more data for analysis.

- As a **Chartered Finance Analyst** (**CFA**), it is my duty to make investment in AI more effective and efficient. The best way to do that is to have hands-on knowledge about technology. If the company/investment project is just copying and pasting code along with a fancy renowned school name, just ignore that and spend your energy somewhere better.

- For **research analysts and management consultants** looking at the banking industry, this is a bottom-up approach to guide you through how exactly we can change banks to be able to run better for a higher return on equity.

- Last but not least, **AI hardware and software developers and researchers**, this can perhaps help you look at common opportunities for your research topics in case you need ideas.

What this book covers

Chapter 1, *The Importance of AI in Banking*, explains what AI is and discusses its applications in banking. This chapter also provides a detailed introduction to banking as a sector, the complexity of banking processes, and diversification in banking functions.

Chapter 2, *Time Series Analysis*, covers time series analysis. This chapter explains time series analysis in detail with examples and explains how the **Machine-to-Machine (M2M)** concept can be helpful in the implementation of time series analysis.

Chapter 3, *Using Features and Reinforcement Learning to Automate Bank Financing*, covers reinforcement learning. It also covers different AI modeling techniques using examples, as well as the business functions of the bank in the context of examples.

Chapter 4, *Mechanizing Capital Market Decisions*, discusses the basic financial and capital market concepts. We will look at how AI can help us optimize the best capital structure by running risk models and generating sales forecasts using macro-economic data. The chapter also covers important machine learning modeling techniques such as learning optimization and linear regression.

Chapter 5, *Predicting the Future of Investment Bankers*, introduces AI techniques followed by auto-syndication for new issues. We will see how capital can be obtained from interested investors. In the latter section of the chapter, we will cover the case of identifying acquirers and targets—a process that requires science to pick the ones that need banking services.

Chapter 6, *Automated Portfolio Management Using Treynor-Black Model and ResNet*, focuses on the dynamics of investors. The chapter discusses portfolio management techniques and explains how to combine them with AI to automate decision-making when buying assets.

Chapter 7, *Sensing Market Sentiment for Algorithmic Marketing at Sell Side*, focuses on the sell side of the financial market. The chapter provides details about securities firms and investment banks. This chapter also discusses sentiment analysis and covers an example of building a network using Neo4j.

Chapter 8, *Building Personal Wealth Advisers with Bank APIs*, focuses on consumer banking. The chapter explains the requirements of managing the digital data of customers. The chapter also explains how to access open bank APIs and explains document layout analysis.

`Chapter 9`, *Mass Customization of Client Lifetime Wealth*, explains how to combine data from the survey for personal data analysis. The chapter also discusses Neo4j, which is a graph database. In this chapter, we will build a chatbot to serve customers 24/7. We will also look at an example entailing the prediction of customer responses using natural language processing, Neo4j, and cipher languages to manipulate data from the Neo4j database.

`Chapter 10`, *Real World Considerations*, serves as a summary of the AI modeling techniques covered in the previous chapters. The chapter also shows where to look for further knowledge of the domain.

To get the most out of this book

Before you get started, I assume that you are running Ubuntu 16.04LTS Desktop or above and have done your Python 101 course. Knowledge of how to install the relevant software packages is assumed and will not be covered in this book.

Three database engines (SQLite, MongoDB, and Neo4j) are used in this book. Please make sure that you have them installed.

Regarding data sources, we will get data from data.world (`https://data.world/`) and a paid subscription to Quandl (Sharadar Core US Equities Bundle (`https://www.quandl.com/databases/SFA/data`) for chapters 4 and 5, and Sharadar Fund Prices (`https://www.quandl.com/databases/SFP/data`) for chapters 6 and 7), Twitter's Premium Search (`https://developer.twitter.com/en/docs/tweets/search/overview/premium`) for chapter 7, and the Open Bank Project (`https://uk.openbankproject.com/`) for chapter 8.

Download the example code files

You can download the example code files for this book from your account at `www.packt.com`. If you purchased this book elsewhere, you can visit `www.packt.com/support` and register to have the files emailed directly to you.

You can download the code files by following these steps:

1. Log in or register at `www.packt.com`.
2. Select the **SUPPORT** tab.
3. Click on **Code Downloads & Errata**.
4. Enter the name of the book in the **Search** box and follow the onscreen instructions.

Once the file is downloaded, please make sure that you unzip or extract the folder using the latest version of:

- WinRAR/7-Zip for Windows
- Zipeg/iZip/UnRarX for Mac
- 7-Zip/PeaZip for Linux

The code bundle for the book is also hosted on GitHub at `https://github.com/PacktPublishing/Hands-On-Artificial-Intelligence-for-Banking`. In case there's an update to the code, it will be updated on the existing GitHub repository.

We also have other code bundles from our rich catalog of books and videos available at `https://github.com/PacktPublishing/`. Check them out!

Download the color images

We also provide a PDF file that has color images of the screenshots/diagrams used in this book. You can download it here: `https://static.packt-cdn.com/downloads/9781788830782_ColorImages.pdf`.

Conventions used

There are a number of text conventions used throughout this book.

`CodeInText`: Indicates code words in text, database table names, folder names, filenames, file extensions, pathnames, dummy URLs, user input, and Twitter handles. Here is an example: "The function will download the price data of any given ticker in the `SHARADAR` database from Quandl."

A block of code is set as follows:

```
#list of key intent, product and attribute
product_list = ['deposit','loan']
attribute_list = ['pricing','balance']
intent_list = ['check']
print('loading nlp model')
nlp = spacy.load('en_core_web_md')
```

Any command-line input or output is written as follows:

```
sudo cp dataset.csv /var/lib/Neo4j/import/edge.csv
sudo cp product.csv /var/lib/Neo4j/import/product.csv
sudo cp customer.csv /var/lib/Neo4j/import/customer.csv
```

Bold: Indicates a new term, an important word, or words that you see onscreen. For example, words in menus or dialog boxes appear in the text like this. Here is an example: "An **asset class** is defined as a group of assets that bear similar characteristics."

 Warnings or important notes appear like this.

 Tips and tricks appear like this.

Get in touch

Feedback from our readers is always welcome.

General feedback: If you have questions about any aspect of this book, mention the book title in the subject of your message and email us at customercare@packtpub.com.

Errata: Although we have taken every care to ensure the accuracy of our content, mistakes do happen. If you have found a mistake in this book, we would be grateful if you would report this to us. Please visit www.packt.com/submit-errata, selecting your book, clicking on the Errata Submission Form link, and entering the details.

Piracy: If you come across any illegal copies of our works in any form on the Internet, we would be grateful if you would provide us with the location address or website name. Please contact us at copyright@packt.com with a link to the material.

If you are interested in becoming an author: If there is a topic that you have expertise in and you are interested in either writing or contributing to a book, please visit authors.packtpub.com.

Reviews

Please leave a review. Once you have read and used this book, why not leave a review on the site that you purchased it from? Potential readers can then see and use your unbiased opinion to make purchase decisions, we at Packt can understand what you think about our products, and our authors can see your feedback on their book. Thank you!

For more information about Packt, please visit packt.com.

Section 1: Quick Review of AI in the Finance Industry

The section gives a general economic and financial overview of the banking industry—which rarely happens in an IT programming book. It exists to give both technologists and business professionals a taste of both sides.

This section comprises the following chapter:

- Chapter 1, *The Importance of AI in Finance*

The Importance of AI in Banking

1

Artificial intelligence, commonly known as **AI**, is a very powerful technology. A thoughtful implementation of AI can do wonders in automating business functions. AI has the power to transform a wide variety of industries through its application. As computer systems have evolved over time, they have become very powerful. Consequently, machines have also become very powerful and can perform many complicated tasks with ease. For example, **Optical Character Recognition** (**OCR**) is a task that even personal computers can perform easily with the help of software. However, OCR requires intelligence to translate dots from an image into characters. So, in an ideal case, OCR will be considered an area of AI. However, because of the power of machines, we tend to not consider it as an application of AI.

In this chapter, our focus is to understand what AI is and its application in banking. Banking is an industry or domain that is extremely diversified and complex. To simplify complex banking functions, the banking industry requires a constant supply of advanced technological solutions. As shown in a recent analysis conducted by Forbes (`https://www.forbes.com/sites/forbestechcouncil/2018/12/05/how-artificial-intelligence-is-helping-financial-institutions/#2e989fae460a`), the implementation of AI in various banking processes will save the industry more than $1 trillion by 2030. Consequently, the banking industry will benefit the most from AI systems in the near future.

We will begin with a brief introduction to AI and banking as an industry. Here, we will define the methods of implementing AI in software systems. We will also learn how the banking industry can benefit from the application of AI. There will be many more topics to cover before we complete this chapter. So, instead of simply discussing what you can expect from this chapter, let's jump straight into it!

In this chapter, we'll focus on the following topics:

- What is AI?
- Understanding the banking sector
- Importance of accessible banking
- Application of AI in banking

What is AI?

AI, also known as **machine intelligence**, is all about creating machines that demonstrate the intelligence that is usually displayed by humans in the form of natural intelligence. John McCarthy coined the term *artificial intelligence* in 1955.

AI has witnessed two winters so far: once in the 1970s with the reduction of funding by the **Defense Advanced Research Projects Agency** or **DARPA** (https://www.darpa.mil/), then known as **ARPA**, and another time with the abandonment of an expert system by major IT corporates such as Texas Instruments (http://www.ti.com/) and Xerox (https://www.xerox.com/).

In a way, AI aids in the process of transferring decision making from humans to machines, based on predefined rules. In the field of computer science, AI is also defined as the study of intelligent agents. An intelligent agent is any device that learns from the environment and makes decisions based on what it has learned to maximize the probability of achieving its predefined goals.

AI is capable of solving an extremely broad range of problems. These problems include, but are not limited to, simple mathematical puzzles, finding the best route from one location to another, understanding human language, and processing huge amounts of research data to produce meaningful reports. The following is a list of capabilities that the system must have in order to solve these problems along with a brief description of what each means:

- **Reasoning**: The ability to solve puzzles and make logic-based deductions
- **Knowledge representation**: The ability to process knowledge collected by researchers and experts
- **Planning**: The ability to set goals and define ways to successfully achieve them
- **Learning**: The ability to improve algorithms by experience
- **Natural Language Processing** (**NLP**): The ability to understand human language

- **Perception**: The ability to use sensors and devices, such as cameras, microphones, and more, in order to acquire enough input to understand and interpret different features of the environment
- **Motion**: The ability to move around

How does a machine learn?

Let's take a quick look at the basics of machine learning. There are three methods that a machine can use in order to learn: supervised learning, unsupervised learning, and reinforcement learning, as described in the following list:

- **Supervised learning** is based on the concept of mining labeled training data. The training data is represented as a pair consisting of the supplied input (also known as a **feature vector**—this is a vector of numbers that can represent the inputted data numerically as features) and the expected output data (also known as **labels**). Each pair is tagged with a label. The following diagram illustrates the supervised learning method:

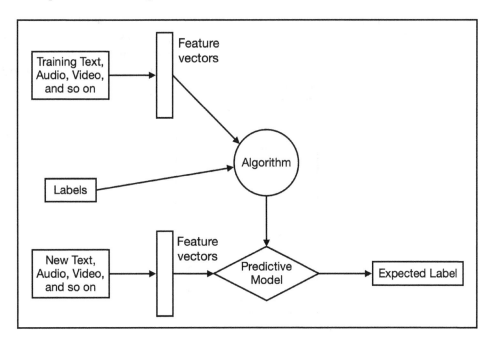

- **Unsupervised learning** is based on a situation where the training data is provided without any underlying information about the data, which means the training data is not labeled. The unsupervised learning algorithm will try to find the hidden meaning for this training data. The following diagram illustrates the unsupervised learning method:

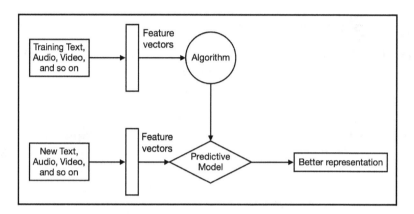

- **Reinforcement learning** is a machine learning technique that does not have training data. This method is based on two things—an agent and a reward for that agent. The agent is expected to draw on its experience in order to get a reward. The following diagram depicts the reinforcement learning method:

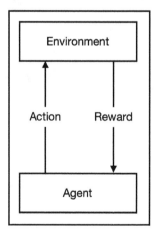

Software requirements for the implementation of AI

The open source movement (which will be discussed in the *Importance of accessible banking* section) propels software development. The movement is coupled with the improvement of hardware (for example, GPU, CPU, storage, and network hardware). It is also supported by countless heroes who work on improving hardware performance and internet connectivity. These technicians have developed the AI algorithm to the point where it delivers near-human performance.

The following diagram depicts the typical technology stack that we should consider whenever we implement software to perform machine learning projects:

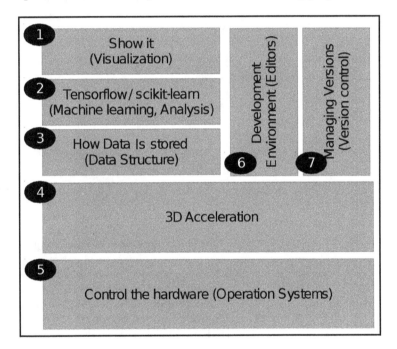

The following table breaks down several key technologies that contribute to the different software components mentioned in the preceding diagram:

Serial no.	Components	Software/package name	Software/package description
1	User interface/application programming interface	API/Python	API: An application programming interface is a type of interface that allows a program to interact with another program using the internet protocol. In comparison to the UI, the API is meant for a robot. It will be used to pull data from data sources throughout the coding chapters of this book, where we will create consumer banking services for an open bank project.
2	Machine learning and analysis	TensorFlow, scikit-learn, and ImageNet	Google's TensorFlow (https://www.tensorflow.org/) has been one of the most popular frameworks for deep learning since 2017. Scikit-learn (https://scikit-learn.org/stable/) is a handy machine learning package that delivers lots of useful functionalities in machine learning pipelines. TensorFlow and Keras (https://keras.io/) will be used when we work on deep neural networks, while we will use scikit-learn in less complex networks and data preparation works. These libraries will be used throughout the book, from chapter 2 to 9, to build machine learning models. ImageNet (http://www.image-net.org/) was created by Princeton University in 2009 to aid researchers in testing and building a deep learning model based on a dataset, which led to flourishing research on image recognition using deep learning networks. We will be converting an image recognition network to identify stock trends in Chapter 6, *Automated Portfolio Management Using Treynor Black Model and ResNet.*

3	Data structure	Pandas and NumPy	Pandas (`https://pandas.pydata.org/`) and NumPy (`http://www.numpy.org/`) are data structures that allow Python to manipulate data. They are used throughout this book's coding samples. These libraries are one of the key reasons for Python's popularity among data scientists. These libraries are used from chapter 2 to 9.
4	3D acceleration	Nvidia	The computation performance of Keras-related coding, such as the coding found in Chapter 3, *Using Features and Reinforcement Learning to Automate Bank Decisions,* will be enhanced if 3D acceleration (such as the software and hardware provided by Nvidia (`https://www.nvidia.com/en-us/`)) is used in the backend by TensorFlow. The driver will help to improve certain elements of GPU performance.
5	Operation systems	Ubuntu	This is a free, open source operating system that is compatible with most of the Python libraries we will use in this book. It is arguably the operating system of choice for the AI community.

6	Programming languages and development environment	Python and IDLE	Python programming is the language of AI. Python's existence is due to funding by DARPA in 1999, which was granted in order to provide a common programming language in a plain, readable style. It is open source. IDLE is a development environment that lies within the Python package. It allows programs to be written, debugged, and run. However, there are many more environments available for developers to code in, such as Jupyter Notebook, Spyder, and more. We will use Python and the **Integrated Development and Learning Environment (IDLE)** for easier code development (you can find them at `https://docs.python.org/3/library/idle.html`).
7	Version control	GitHub	GitHub is one of the most popular cloud-based collaboration sites. It was made possible because of the proliferation of cloud technologies, which enable scalable computing and storage. This is where our code base will be housed and exchanged.

With our brief introduction to the tools, technologies, and packages that we will use throughout the course of this book complete, let's now move on to explore an important area of AI—deep learning. The following section will explain deep learning and neural networks in detail.

Neural networks and deep learning

In addition to the open source movement, research breakthroughs in neural networks have played a big role in improving the accuracy of decision making in AI algorithms. You can refer to *Deep Learning* (`https://www.deeplearningbook.org/`) by Ian Goodfellow, Yoshua Benjio, and Aaron Courville for a more mathematical and formal introduction, and you can refer to *Deep Learning with Keras* (`https://www.packtpub.com/big-data-and-business-intelligence/deep-learning-keras?utm_source=githubutm_medium=repositoryutm_campaign=9781787128422`) by Antonio Gulli and Sujit Pal for a concise analysis for developers.

Deep learning is a special subfield or branch of machine learning. The deep learning methodology is inspired by a computer system that is modeled on the human brain, known as a **neural network**.

Online customer support by banks via a mobile or web application chatbot is an excellent example of deep learning in banking. Such applications (that is, chatbots) are powerful when it comes to understanding the context of customer requests, preferences, and interests. The chatbot is connected to backend applications that interact with data stores. Based on the customer's inputs or selection of services, the chatbot presents to the customer various alternative sub-services to choose from.

The chatbot or deep learning applications work in layers. It can be compared to learning a language. For instance, once a person masters the alphabet by rigorously learning how to identify each letter uniquely, they will be eligible to move on to the next layer of complexity—words. The person will start learning small words and then long words. Upon mastering words, the person will start forming sentences, understanding grammatical concepts at different layers of complexity. Once they reach the top of this hierarchy of layers of complexity, the person will be able to master the language.

You might have noticed that in each phase or layer of the hierarchy, the learning becomes more complex. Each layer is built based on the learning or knowledge gathered from the previous layer of complexity. This is how deep learning works. The program keeps on learning, forming more knowledge with new layers of complexity based on the knowledge received from the previous layer. The layered complexity is where the word *deep* was taken from. Deep learning is a type of unsupervised learning, so it is much faster than supervised learning.

The major impact of deep learning is that the performance of the model is better as it can accommodate more complex reasoning. We want financial decisions to be made accurately. This means that it will be more cost-effective to give the shareholders of banks a reasonable return while balancing the interests of the bank's clients.

What we expect from a smart machine is as simple as **input**, **process**, and **output**, as shown in the following diagram:

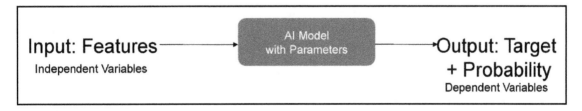

In most financial use cases, we deploy supervised learning, which resembles the process of training an animal—here, you provide a reward for a correct outcome and discourage an incorrect outcome. That's why we need to have the outcome (that is, the target variable) for training to happen.

Hardware requirements for the implementation of AI

While setting the budget for the hardware required by a bank, you need to ensure that it encapsulates the right configurations. This will allow you to deliver the promised results in terms of financial results or time to market, especially now that you are about to start a bank from scratch!

You'd better be sure that every penny works, given that the economic pressures on banks are pretty high. In order to do any of this, we need to understand the contribution that hardware makes to AI in order to ensure we have the right resources.

Graphics processing units

Besides the software and algorithms, the use of a **Graphics Processing Unit (GPU)** and **Solid-State Drive (SSD)** helps to speed up machine learning. The use of GPUs and SSDs makes it possible for a computer to think intelligently.

A GPU is a specially designed circuit that can process calculations in a parallel manner. This applies to computer graphic processing, where each of the pixels needs to be processed simultaneously in order to produce a full picture. To visualize this, suppose that there are 10 pixels to be processed. We can either process each of the 10 pixels one by one, or we can process them in 10 processes simultaneously.

The CPU has the unique strength of having a fast processing time per pixel, while the GPU has the strength of multiple threads to handle flat data all at once. Both CPUs and GPUs can do parallel data processing with varying degrees. The following table shows the difference between sequential and parallel data processing:

Sequential data processing	Parallel data processing
Data comes in sequences, which requires a longer time to complete the computation.	Data comes in parallel, which improves the processing time.

Aside from being great at processing images, a GPU is also leveraged for deep learning. Although deep learning describes the number of layers the neural network has, deep neural networks are often characterized as having a wide record and lots of variables to describe the input.

When used in combination with a GPU, the SSD also improves the speed to read and write data to the CPU/GPU for processing.

Solid-state drives

Another hardware requirement for machine learning is a storage device called an SSD. The traditional hard disk has a mechanical motor to place the head that reads or writes data at a designated location on the magnetic tape or disk. In contrast to this, the SSD reads and writes data using an electric current on a circuit without the movement of a motor. Comparing the mechanical movement of motors with the electric current onboard, an SSD has a data retrieval speed that is 20 times faster.

For students in operation research, comparing the two is as simple as identifying the hardware capacity, which is akin to how we design a factory—find the capacity and reduce the bottlenecks as much as possible!

Modeling approach—CRISP-DM

CRISP-DM refers to a **cross-industry standard process for data mining**. Data mining is the process of exploring large amounts of data to identify any patterns to be applied to the next set of data to generate the desired output. To create the models in this book, we will use the CRISP-DM modeling approach. This will help us to maintain a uniform method of implementing machine learning projects. The following diagram depicts the project execution using the CRISP-DM approach in a machine learning project:

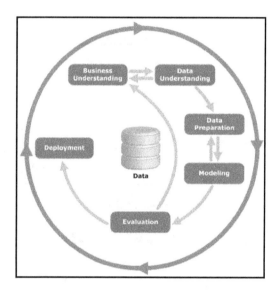

As you can see in the preceding diagram, there are various phases of the CRISP-DM approach. We can explain them in detail, as follows:

1. **Business Understanding**: This phase involves defining the business objectives for the project. During this phase, you clarify the queries related to the core business objectives. For example, a core business objective may be to predict when the customers leave a particular website using the historical data of the customer's interaction with the website. The relevant query to clarify might be whether the payment interface currently in place is the reason for customers navigating off the website. Business success criteria are also laid out during this phase of the project execution.

2. **Data Understanding**: This phase involves understanding historical data that is mined in the database or data store. The data is analyzed for its size, format, quantity, number of records, significance in relation to business, fields, source of data, and more.

3. **Data Preparation**: This phase involves raising the quality of the data to the level required for the machine learning algorithms to process it. Examples of data preparation include formatting data in the desired format, rounding the numbers to an acceptable degree of precision, and preparing derived attributes.

4. **Modeling**: This phase involves selecting a modeling technique or algorithm to be applied. A modeling algorithm is used to find a function that, when applied to an input, produces the desired output.

5. **Evaluation**: This phase involves assessing the accuracy of the training model that was built in the previous phase. Any required revisions to the model are made in order to increase efficiency and accuracy.

6. **Deployment**: This phase involves defining a deployment strategy for the training model in the live environment to work on new data. The models are monitored for accuracy.

After roughly covering what AI is, how machines learn, and the methods of AI implementation, it is now time to look at banking as a sector or industry. In the following section, we will explore the various types of banking and the challenges involved in the banking sector.

Understanding the banking sector

The banking sector is defined as a devoted economy for holding specific types of financial assets using methods that will make said assets grow financially over a period of time. Banking sectors are governed by rules imposed by governments or similar bodies.

Renowned author and financial consultant Stephen Valdez described in his work, *Introduction to Global Financial Markets* (please visit `https://www.macmillanihe.com/companion/Valdez-Introduction-To-Global-Financial-Markets-8th-Edition/about-this-book/`), the different types of banking in the global financial markets. These are commercial banking, investment banking, securities firms, asset management, insurance, and shadow banking.

These types of banking are required to fulfill the needs of a wide variety of customers, ranging from large organizations to individual customers. The following is a description of these various types of banking based on the needs of customers:

- **Commercial banking** can be retail (serving consumers) or wholesale (serving companies). Essentially, banks focus on taking deposits from savers and lending them to borrowers by charging interest. Commercial banks thrive on their ability to assess the riskiness of the loan extended to borrowers. Any failure to accurately assess the risk can lead to bankruptcy due to the failure to return money to the depositors. Many banks have failed in financial crises, including Washington Mutual in the US.
- **Investment banking** includes advisory businesses and security trading businesses. Advisory businesses deal with the buying and selling of companies, also known as **mergers and acquisitions (M&A)**, debt and equity capital raising (for example, listing companies on the New York Stock Exchange), and security trading businesses. The security trading businesses deal with the trading of stocks, fixed income, commodities, and currencies. Securities trading involves a buyer who is willing to buy a security, a seller who is willing to sell a security, and a broker who facilitates the buying and selling of a security.

The advisory businesses hinge on creating value for companies by combining or spinning off businesses. This process optimizes the organizational performance for M&A activities. It also optimizes the cost of capital for clients into a standardized borrowing structure (such as bonds). The clients can do more investment by issuing new shares or canceling existing company shares (equity) to financial market participants.

All of the aforementioned activities create value with the correct evaluation of the companies given by the participants of the markets, which are driven by moods and more rational concerns.

- **Asset management** includes funds of all kinds—mutual funds, exchange-traded funds, hedge funds, private equity, and more. Asset management companies invest in various types of financial assets and the various life stages of a corporation using different investment strategies (a combination of buying and selling decisions). A critical decision made in this industry also falls under the umbrella of proper valuation, with regard to an investment's future values.

Asset management participants have a hunger for generating returns to meet various purposes, from the protection of asset values to appreciation. They are typically referred to as the **buy side**, which represents the asset owners, while the banking services that help the buy side are referred to as the **sell side**, which typically includes securities sales (client-facing, gathering orders), trading (executing the orders), and research (evaluating the securities).

- **Insurance** includes general insurance and life insurance. Life insurance protects buyers from mortality risks (consequences of death), and non-life insurance covers everything else, such as loss due to disasters, the loss of luggage, the loss of rockets (for example, Elon Musk's SpaceX loss) and vessels, system breaches due to hacking or viruses, and more.

The core function of insurance is to estimate the risk profile of borrowers. On the other hand, the ability to generate investment returns to cover losses can be important as well. The stronger the investment performance of the insurer, the more aggressive the pricing of insurance it can offer and the more competitive it becomes. That's one of the reasons why Berkshire Hathaway can provide competitive insurance pricing—due to its superior investment performance.

- **Consumer banking** is represented by the asset size of consumer debts, which focuses on the mortgage, auto, and personal loans, and credit card businesses that we might need at various points in our life.
- **Shadow banking** is a lending settlement involving activities outside the regular banking system. It refers to alternative investment funds, such as bitcoin investment funds, broker-dealers in securities, and consumer and mortgage finance companies that provide lending to consumers.

The size of banking relative to the world's economies

By comparing the sheer size of the finance industry with the world's annual income from production, we get a fair sense of how the world uses banking services to support itself. However, it is rather abstract to only show the statistics. Let's say the world is a person. How does finance fit into this person's life? The following is a list of points to consider:

- **Annual income**: The productivity and, therefore, income of the global economy as gauged by the World Bank was $86 trillion in 2018. Roughly, one-fifth (19%) of the annual income comes from trading across borders (where export trade volume is at $15 trillion).
- **Wealth**: The global person has approximately 4.4 years equivalent of annual income (annual GDP). A breakdown of the annual GDP can be found in the table at the end of this section. The information on annual income has been derived from various sources by comparing the activities with the size of the GDP. These 4.6 years can be bifurcated as follows:
  - 0.9 years has been with the asset manager.
  - 0.9 years has been deposited in banks.
  - 0.8 years has been in the stock markets.
  - 2.3 years has been funded by credit/borrowing (1.17 through debts, 1.0 through bank loans, 0.5 through shadow banks, and 0.03 through consumer credits).

  Of course, this is a simplified treatment of global wealth; some figures could be double-counted, and the stock market figure could include deposits placed by listed companies that are accounted for by bank liabilities. However, given that we want to understand the relative size of various financial activities and their importance, we've just taken a shortcut to show the figures as they are.

- **Insurance**: To protect against any kind of undesirable risks derived from productive or investment activities, 6% of the global person's annual income was spent on the insurance that covers 1.45 times their equivalent income. The premium will be used to buy the underlying financial assets to generate income to offset any undesirable risks.
- **Derivatives**: As a risk-protection instrument, besides buying insurance, banks can also offer derivatives as a financial instrument to offer risk protection. The term *derivatives* refer to the agreement between two parties to pay or receive economic benefits under certain conditions of underlying assets. The underlying assets vary from **fixed income** and **currency** to **commodities** (**FICC**).

Fixed income includes the interest rate and credit derivatives. Currency refers to foreign exchange derivatives, and commodities refer to commodity derivatives. Foreign exchange came in second with $87 trillion of outstanding exposure, which is roughly equal to the world's GDP. Commodity, credit, and equity derivatives have smaller shares, with each at around 2% to 9% equivalent of GDP. When accounting for derivatives as a risk-protection instrument, we exclude a form of derivatives called the interest rate **over-the-counter** (**OTC**), which is equal to 6 times the annual income—this is far more than the annual income that our wealth requires for protection. Indeed, some investors take the interest rate OTC as an investment. We carve out this instrument for our overall understanding of insurance. OTC refers to the bilateral agreements between banks and bank customers.

Another form of agreement can be exchange-traded agreements, referring to bank customers buying and selling products via a centralized exchange. I did not include too many exchange-traded figures, but the figures mentioned in this point for foreign exchange, commodity, credit and equity, and so on, serve the purpose of showing the relative size of the sectors.

The following table lists the GDP figures:

	Trillions in USD in 2018	% of GDP
Income	75.87	100%
World's GDP (annual income generated globally)	75.87	100.00%
Global export volume	14.64	19.00%
Wealth	332.46	438%
Global asset management	69.1	91.00%
Global bank liabilities (including deposits)	58.93	78.00%
Global stock markets	79.24	104.00%
Global debt markets	57.49	76.00%
Bank loans	29.7	39.00%
Shadow banking	34	45.00%
Global Consumer Debt	4	5.00%
Global insurance (new premium written)	4.73	**6.00%**
Insurance coverage—derivatives (ex-interest rate OTC)	110.15	**145.00%**
Global foreign exchange OTC + exchange-traded derivatives	87.41	115.00%
Commodity OTC contracts	1.86	2.00%

Credit OTC derivatives	9.58	13.00%
Equity-linked contracts	6.57	9.00%
Interest rate OTC contracts	461.98	609.00%

All figures were earlier reported for the full-year figures of 2018 unless otherwise stated. GDP and stock market sizes are from the World Bank; export trade data is from the World Trade Organization; new insurance premium figures are from Swiss Re Sigma for 2018; the global asset management size is from BCG Global Asset Management for 2018; all banking, debts, and derivatives statistics are from the Bank for International Settlements.

Customers in banking

Customers in the finance industry include depositors and borrowers engaged in saving and lending activities. When engaging in commercial banking activities, such as cross-border payment or trade finance, they are called **applicants** (senders of funds) and **beneficiaries** (receivers of funds).

If customers are engaged in investment banking, securities, and asset management activities, they are called **investors** or, generally, **clients**. To protect buyers of insurance products from potential risks, the person buying is called the **proposer**, and the item is called an **insured item**. In cases where risk occurs and if/when compensation is required from the insurers, the person to be compensated is called a **beneficiary**.

Non-financial corporations are the real corporate clients of all financial activities and should be considered the real players of economics. They save excess cash and produce goods and services for consumers.

A message that I wish to clearly underline and highlight is that finance is a service to real economies. So why does financial sector growth surpass real economic growth? Well, as per the opinion of Cecchetti and Kharroubi, too much finance damages the real growth of economics. That is, it takes away high-quality research and development talents that could contribute to real economies. Therefore, the taking away of talented people negatively impacts production factors. You can find out more about this at https://www.bis.org/publ/work490.pdf.

Importance of accessible banking

Like electricity and water, banking should be made as widely and easily available as utilities. Only when we make banks efficient can we make them accessible and have them benefit the highest number of people possible. Banking is a service that is provided to make the best use of capital/money to generate returns for those who save and/or those who need the capital to have a more productive life at an agreed risk and return.

What we want to do is to be consistent with Robert J. Shiller's sentiment in his book, *Finance and the Good Society*, where he indicates the necessity of information technology in finance to help achieve our goals. A step further would be to leverage open source methods and applications to solve the accessibility challenges of the banking industry. Open source software solutions tend to be cost-effective, robust, and secure.

To make banking accessible, one of the most important things to do is to have a lot of data. This will make decisions more efficient and transparent, which can help to reduce the cost of banking decisions. We will discuss the need for open source data in the next section. By virtue of the competitive banking market, the price of banking services will gradually decrease as banks with good efficiency will win a large market share.

Once implemented in the financial sector, AI will have three impacts on the sector—the job of repetitive tasks will be eliminated, there will be increased efficiency with AI augmenting human, and job creation with new AI-related tasks such as model building. Out of these three, job reduction and increased efficiency will impact existing jobs, whereas job creation will have an impact on future talent and the job market.

As automation and efficiency increase, existing jobs will be altered and impacted. Machines will perform day-to-day tasks with more efficiency than humans can. However, to manage, monitor, maintain, and enhance tasks performed by machines or AI, the industry will become open to skilled, techno-functional professionals who understand both banking and AI technology.

Open source software and data

The speed of technological development in the past 20 years or so has been quite rapid due to the open source movement. It started with Linux and was followed by ImageNet. ImageNet provided lots of training data. This training data fueled the activities of technicians who worked in research on developing AI algorithms. These technicians developed algorithms for deep learning and neural networks using open source libraries written in programming languages such as Python, R, scikit-learn, TensorFlow, and more.

While the open source approach encourages software development, another key ingredient of AI is data. Finding practical open data is a challenge. Banks, on the other hand, have the challenge of converting data into a machine-trainable dataset cautiously and safely to make sure that there is no breach of data that customers entrusted the bank with.

Today, in the finance and banking world, client confidentiality remains a key obstacle to opening up data for wider research communities. Real-world problems can be more complex than what we have seen in the open data space. Opening up data stored in databases can be a practical step, while opening up images, such as documents, audio files, or voice dialogues, for example, can be challenging as this data, once masked or altered, may lose some information systematically.

In fact, the major cost of implementing real-life applications in banking also comes from the data-feed subscription. The cost of data collection and aggregation is a major challenge that you will see in this book. How our society is handling this problem and incentivizing the commercial sector to tackle it requires further discussion beyond the scope of this book. Following this same spirit, the code for this book is open source.

Why do we need AI if a good banker can do the job?

Let's consider a single financial task of matching demand for capital in the funding markets. This is a highly routine task of matching numbers. Here, it is obvious that the computer would be a better fit for the job.

The goal of employing AI is to make machines do the things that humans do right now, but with more efficiency. Many people wonder whether applying AI in banking might affect the jobs of those working in the industry.

Do remember that the aim is not to replace humans, but to augment the current human capacity to improve productivity, which has been the goal of technology throughout the history of human civilization. Humans are known to be weaker in determining accurate probability, as shown in the psychological research paper, *Thinking, Fast and Slow*, April 2, 2013, by Daniel Kahneman. Therefore, it is challenging to make a probability decision without a computer.

Applications of AI in banking

According to the McKinsey Global Institute (`https://www.mckinsey.com/~/media/ mckinsey/industries/advanced%20electronics/our%20insights/ how%20artificial%20intelligence%20can%20deliver%20real%20value%20to%20companies /mgi-artificial-intelligence-discussion-paper.ashx`), out of 13 industries, financial services ranked third in AI adoption, followed by the high-tech, telecommunications, and automotive and assembly industries.

As the Mckinsey report does not mention the use case in banking, with a bit of research, perhaps we can take a look at the four ways in which AI creates values, as shown in the following list:

- **Project**: Forecast and anticipate demand, improve sourcing, and reduce inventory (capital).
- **Produce**: Provide services at a lower cost or higher quality.
- **Promote**: Provide offers for the right price with the right message for the right customers at the right time.
- **Provide**: Rich, personal, and convenient user experiences.

Let's examine how each finance participant applies AI to the following aspects, as shown in the following table:

Participants	Project: better forecast	Produce: lower processing cost	Promote: personalized offer	Provide: convenience
Commercial banks	Optimize funding needs.	Using AI, trade finance processing can be automated, which will result in increased efficiency.	AI can provide a real-time quotation of export/import financing as the goods move to different stakeholders with different types and levels of risk.	Improve client services with an NLP-enabled chatbot.

Investment banks	Valuation of corporations.	With AI, it becomes faster and cheaper to reach the market signal by identifying the market's sentiments.	AI can match the needs of asset sellers and buyers through automated matching.	Mobile workforce with access to information at any time.
Asset management	Asset valuation and optimization.	AI can help here by automating trading and portfolio balancing.	AI can recommend investments to customers.	Fast and convenient portfolio updates.
Consumer banks	Project a realistic savings plan.	Personalized bot advisers can capture the data from receipts without human help.	AI can understand the right time at which consumers need financing or investment products.	Serve clients 24/7 anywhere using smart bots.

Across the board, we can now see how data is being leveraged for smart decision making in the field of finance: more data points and a higher speed of exchange can lead to a much lower cost of finance. More detailed examples will be provided in the following chapters.

How do we attain this lower cost? Essentially, we get it by having fewer hours spent working on producing an aspect of the banking service.

Impact of AI on a bank's profitability

To give you an idea of AI's impact on a bank's profitability, let's take a look at some simple estimates from two perspectives: the improvement of model accuracy and the time spent to run/train the model.

Over the past 10 years, the clock rate and the number of cores have improved tenfold, from around 300 cores to around 3,000 cores.

I have compared the shallow machine learning or statistical model I experienced a decade ago to what I see today with deep neural networks. The model accuracy of neural networks improves the model from around 80% to over 90%, with a 12.5% rate of improvement. The following table shows improvements in the memory data rate, bus width, and size:

Year	Processors	Core clock	Memory data rate	Memory bus width	Memory size
2007	8800 Ultra[42]	612 MHz	2.16 GHz	384 bit	768 MB
2018	Titan X[43]	1417 MHz	10 GHz	384 bit	12 GB
2018	GeForce RTX 2080 Ti	1545 MHz	14 GHz	352 bit	11 GB GDDR6

The following table highlights the improvement in the areas of banking:

Areas	Improvement	Areas of banking
Project: better forecast	Model forecast accuracy improves by 15%.	Risk model, pricing
Produce: lower processing cost	Automation rate of 50%.	Operations
Promote: personalized offers	Model forecast accuracy improves by 15%.	Risk model, pricing
Provide: convenience	Reduces delay by 50% if all processes are automated.	Operations

If the cost-to-income ratio is around 70% for banks, then the automation rate will likely reduce the ratios by half to 35%. However, the cost of technology investment will take up another 5-10%, taking the target cost-to-income ratios from 40% to 45% following the proliferation of AI in banking. This will impact the banks in developed countries more, as the cost of labor is quite high compared to emerging markets.

Improving the accuracy of forecasts will reduce the cost of the bank's forecast ability further, which, in turn, will reduce the cost of risk by 15%. My personal view is that, for developed countries, the cost of risk is at 50 **basis points** (**bps**) of the overall asset; a reduction of 15% on the bank's cost of risk cannot have a significant impact on their profitability.

The improvement in forecast accuracy and convenience will improve the accessibility of banks, which means they can reach a bigger market that was not considered feasible in the past. That is, the profitability ratio of return on the equity does not reflect the impact; rather, it will be shown in the size of the bank and the market capitalization of banks. It should generate an improvement of 15% given a wider reach.

All in all, there is an improvement in return by 80%, from 7.9% **Return on Equity** (**ROE**) to 14.5%. However, there will be additional capital requirements for systemically important banks from 11% to 12%, gradually, which will drag the overall ROE down to 13.3% in the target AI adaption stage, with all regulations settling in.

Summary

We began this chapter by explaining what AI is all about. AI is the technology that makes machines perform tasks that humans can do, such as weather prediction, budget forecasting, and more. It enables machines to learn based on data. We looked at the various techniques of AI, such as machine learning and deep learning. Later, we looked at the complex processes of the banking domain. If we can automate them, we can reduce costs in the banking sector. We also learned about the importance of accessible banking. Later, we looked at the application of AI in the banking sector and its positive impact, with a few numbers to support it.

In the next chapter, we will continue our journey of AI in banking. As a next step, the chapter will focus on time series analysis and forecasting. It will use various Python libraries, such as scikit-learn, to perform time series analysis. The chapter will also explain how to measure the accuracy of machine learning-based forecasting. The chapter will be full of interesting content and will teach you how to combine financial ratios with machine learning models. This will provide a more in-depth look into how machine learning models can be applied to solve banking problems.

Section 2: Machine Learning Algorithms and Hands-on Examples

2

In this section, we will go through the applications of AI in various businesses and functions of the banking industry. The last chapter is the practical yet theoretical chapter in which I will share how I came up with the features and areas of AI applications in the field of finance. It is important for an AI engineer to develop a model with the right features, yet not get too technical in terms of programming, as it can serve as a timeless guide on how to select the appropriate features regardless of the technology.

This section comprises the following chapters:

Time Series Analysis 2

In the previous chapter, we introduced AI, machine learning, and deep learning. We also discovered how the banking sector functions and how the use of AI can enhance banking processes. We learned the importance of banking processes being easily accessible. We also learned about a machine learning modeling approach called **CRISP-DM**. Overall, the chapter provided the necessary background for the application of machine learning in the banking industry to solve various business problems.

In this chapter, we will learn about an algorithm that analyzes historical data to forecast future behavior, known as **time series analysis**. Time series analysis works on the basis of one variable—time. It is the process of capturing data points, also known as **observations**, at specific time intervals. The goal of this chapter is to understand time series analysis in detail through examples and explain how **Machine-to-Machine** (**M2M**) communication can be helpful in the implementation of time series analysis. We will also understand the concepts of financial banking as well.

In this chapter, we will cover the following topics :

- Understanding time series analysis
- M2M communication
- The basic concepts of financial banking
- AI modeling techniques
- Demand forecasting using time series analysis
- Procuring commodities using neural networks on Keras

Understanding time series analysis

A **time series** is technically defined as the ordered sequence of values of a variable captured over a uniformly spaced time interval. Put simply, it is the method of capturing the value of a variable at specific time intervals. It can be 1 hour, 1 day, or 20 minutes. The captured values of a variable are also known as **data points**. Time series analysis is performed in order to understand the structure of the underlying sources that produced the data. It is also used in forecasting, feedforward control, monitoring, and feedback. The following is a list of some of the known applications of time series analysis:

- Utility studies
- Stock market analysis
- Weather forecasting
- Sales projections
- Workload scheduling
- Expenses forecasting
- Budget analysis

Time series analysis is achieved by applying various analytical methods to extract meaningful information from raw data that has been captured from various data sources. Time series analysis is also useful for producing statistics and other characteristics of data—for example, the size of data, the type of data, the frequency of data, and more. In time series analysis, the capturing of a value is done at a point of observation.

Let's try to understand this through an example. When using time series analysis modeling, the branch manager of a specific branch can predict or forecast the expenses that will occur in the upcoming year. The branch manager can do this by employing a time series analysis machine learning model and then training the model using historical yearly expense records. The recorded observations can be plotted on a graph with a specific time (each day, in this example) on the x axis and historical expenses on the y axis. Therefore, time series analysis is an algorithm that is used to forecast the future values of one variable (that is, yearly expenses in this example) based on the values captured for another variable (in this case, time).

Let's understand this in more detail using another example. In this example, we will imagine that a bank wants to perform expense projections based on the historical data it has. The bank manager wants to know and forecast the expenses in the year 2020 for the branch that he manages. So, the process of forecasting the expenses will start by collecting historical expenses information from the year 2000. First, the bank manager will look at the expenses data for the year.

As we mentioned earlier, time series analysis is done by capturing the values of a variable. Can you guess the variable in this example? I am sure that you will have guessed it by now. The variable under observation is the total expense amount per year. Let's assume that the following is the data per year:

Year	Total expense (in USD)
2000	20,000
2001	22,500
2002	21,000
2003	18,000
2004	25,700
2005	22,100
2006	23,300
2007	17,600
2008	18,200
2009	20,400
2010	21,200
2011	20,900
2012	22,600
2013	17,500
2014	19,300
2015	20,100
2016	22,200
2017	22,500
2018	19,400
2019	23,800

Many options are available to analyze this data and predict future expenses. The analytical methods vary in terms of complexity. The simplest one will be to average out the expenses and assume the resultant value to be the number of expenses for the year 2020. However, this is solely for the purpose of our example. You can find the average of expenses by using various other mathematical and analytical methods as well. With this option, the total number of expenses for the year 2020 will be $20,915.

The complex method may involve analyzing detailed expenses, predicting future values for each individual expense type, and deriving the total expenses amount based on it. This may provide a more accurate prediction than the averaging option. You can apply a more complex analytical method based on your needs. This example is provided so that you can understand how time series analysis works. The amount of historical data that we have used in this example is very limited. AI and machine learning algorithms use large amounts of data to generate predictions or results. The following is a graphical representation of this example:

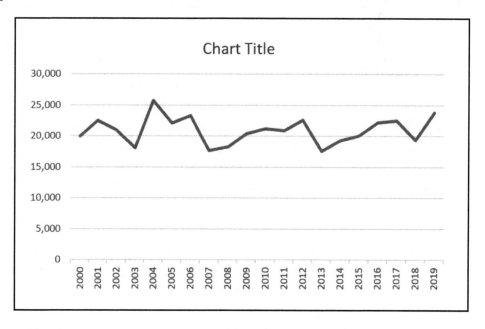

In the following section, we will learn how machines can communicate with each other using a concept known as **M2M communication**.

M2M communication

M2M communication is extremely powerful and can dramatically improve the functions of commercial banking.

M2M communication represents the communication between two machines or devices through various channels such as physical networks, information-sharing networks, software communication, and application interfaces. The sole purpose of M2M communication is the exchange of information across two or more machines or between software running on those machines.

The concept of M2M communication assumes that no human intervention is required while exchanging information between machines. M2M communication can also take place over wireless networks. Wireless networks have made M2M communication easier and more accessible. The following list includes several common applications of M2M communication:

- Manufacturing
- Smart utility management
- Home appliances
- Healthcare device management

However, M2M communication is different from IoT. IoT uses sensors to trigger inputs, whereas M2M communication specifically refers to the interaction between two systems.

Commercial banking is a group of financial services that includes deposits, checking account services, loan services, drafts, certificates of deposits, and savings accounts for individuals and businesses. Commercial banks are the usual destination for peoples' banking needs. *But how do banks function and make money?* This is a very common question that we will answer right now. Commercial banks make money when they earn interest from various types of loans that they provide to their customers. The types of loans can vary, for example, automobile loans, business loans, personal loans, and mortgage loans. Usually, a commercial bank has a specialty in one or more types of loans.

Commercial banks get their capital from various types of account services that they provide to their customers. The types of accounts include checking accounts, savings accounts, corporate accounts, money market accounts, and more. Banks utilize this capital to invest in high-return investment options such as mutual funds, stocks, and bonds. Banks have to pay interest to those customers who have their accounts with the bank. The rate of interest is far less when compared to loans, however.

The role of M2M communication in commercial banking

Consider an example that involves transferring money from one customer's account to another customer's account. In the past, this was a manual task that required filling in an appropriate form, submitting the form to the appropriate department where ledger entries were created, and then the amount was debited from one account and credited to the beneficiary's account.

Nowadays, this process has changed entirely. With a mobile phone, the customer can transfer funds from one account to another without any hassle. The beneficiary's account will be credited with the money within a few minutes. Incredible, isn't it? So, how did this happen? Well, M2M communication and process automation have played a major role in making this happen. It has become possible for machines (that is, computer systems, cloud-based virtual machines, and mobile devices) to connect over a wireless or wired network and transfer every piece of necessary information to another machine or software running on that machine. Nowadays, you only have to visit the bank for a few specific reasons. Customers can now even open a savings bank account or a loan account straight from their mobile devices.

The basic concepts of financial banking

Before we move full steam ahead into another example, we will first craft out our data, AI, and business techniques and knowledge. If you are familiar with all of these concepts, feel free to skip this section.

Financial knowledge is a good place to start to understand how our decisions in forecasting business activities impact financial decision-making in non-financial firms. Additionally, when predicting future activities using a machine learning model, we also learn how the finance industry can prepare for this future volume of business. What financing does to help with core business activities in non-financial firms is covered in the following section.

The functions of financial markets – spot and future pricing

Financial markets, such as exchanges, play the role of markets for products to be exchanged. For example, consider commodities such as natural gas—we can either buy it directly from sellers or buy it via an exchange. As it turns out, long-running economics theories encourage you to buy the product from an exchange as much as possible if the product is standardized. **Chicago Mercantile Exchange** (**CME**) in the US could be a popular choice for commodities and, needless to say, the **New York Stock Exchange** (**NYSE**) is the market for publicly listed equities.

In this chapter, let's stick to natural gas as a product that we need. Of course, in some cases, it could be more efficient to buy it from big oil companies such as Shell—that is, if we want these physical goods from producers on a regular basis.

Within exchange markets, there are two prices— the spot price and the future price. **Spot price** means you can have goods (delivered) now if you pay; **future price** means you get the goods later by paying now.

Choosing between a physical delivery and cash settlement

Even if a change in ownership is to take place, it could occur in two forms, that is, via physical delivery or a cash settlement. Ultimately, physical delivery or a cash settlement depends on whether we need the goods immediately or not. However, on any given trading day, we must weigh up the cost of only two options: *physical delivery (cost of natural gas + cost of financing + cost of storage) as opposed to a cash settlement.*

Essentially, we have four options, as presented in the following table—assuming that we need to have the physical natural gas product in 3 months time for the generation of electricity:

	Physical delivery	Cash settlement
Spot	Finance the purchase to get the product now; store it for 3 months.	Buy the product now and own it on paper. There is no need to keep the goods.
Future	Finance the purchase now to get the product in the future; get it in 3 months.	Finance to buy the product in the future. 3 months later, purchase on spot from the market with physical delivery.

To weigh up the options, we require the following data:

- **Storage costs** should be provided by the internal source if the company owns the storage facility for natural gas. It is assumed to be rather static, for example, at around 0.12 per MMBtu. MMBtu is a unit used to measure the energy content in fuel. It stands for one **Million British Thermal Units**.
- The **financing cost** should cover the storage period and the interest expenses for the purchase cost. It is assumed to be $0.1 per MMBtu. This should be fed by the bank.
- The **cost of natural gas** (spot price) should be provided by the market data provider. The real-time Henry Hub spot price should be provided by Thomson Reuters, for example, at around $2.5 per MMBtu.
- The **cost of futures** should be provided by CME. Data should be available on Quandl free of charge. It should be around $3 per MMBtu for 3-month contract.

The numbers given here merely provide an indication of the magnitude of values. Of course, they could be optimized by comparing the options—however, the decisions can be derived by linear algebra, and not many machine learning techniques are needed. In real life, we should not impose a machine learning solution on anything if we can have a nice deterministic formula to do so.

Options to hedge price risk

To avoid the price swinging outside the predefined price range of natural gas, we will need heuristic rules such as deciding what to do at what price given a fixed target purchase quantity. Alternatively, we need the rules to adjust what has been already placed to sell or buy more.

Take the following example. If the price is beyond the acceptable range, for example, lower than $2.84 or higher than $3.95, we can choose to pocket the profit by doing one of the following:

- Writing options (selling insurance) if the price drops a lot.
- Reducing the loss by buying options (buying insurance) if the price shoots up unfavorably.

The following diagram shows the per-unit payoff from the hedged position by buying insurance against the high procurement price and selling the benefits at a low procurement price:

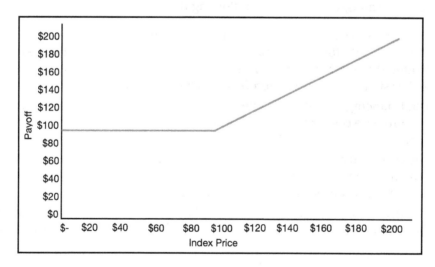

Here, we have sold insurance at an extremely low price—which means that even though we should have enjoyed a lower cost of procurement, we gave it away at the benefit of taking an insurance premium. On the other hand, there will be positive payoff when the price is too expensive, that may eat into the profitability of the company—by paying a premium to buy insurance. The exact price of the insurance is called option pricing and will be addressed in `Chapter 7`, *Sensing Market Sentiment for Algorithmic Marketing at Sell Side*. We now assume that the price we pay for the insurance is the same as the price we earn from selling insurance.

AI modeling techniques

In the following sections, we will introduce the **Autoregressive Integrated Moving Average (ARIMA)**, the most traditional type of forecasting model. We will also introduce a neural network model. ARIMA is a class of statistical models that is used to forecast a time series using past values. ARIMA is an acronym for the following:

- **AR** (**autoregression**): Autoregression is a process that takes previous data values as inputs, applies this to the regression equation, and generates resultant prediction-based data values.
- **I** (**integrated**): ARIMA uses an integrated approach by using differences in observations to make the time series equally spaced. This is done by subtracting the observation from an observation on a previous step or time value.
- **MA** (**moving average**): A model that uses the observation and the residual error applied to past observations.

Introducing the time series model – ARIMA

For this project, we will fit data into a time series model called **ARIMA**. ARIMA is a specific type of time series model in statistics, which is commonly used to predict data points in the future, with parameters on autoregressive terms (p), non-seasonal differences (d), and lagged terms (q).

This ARIMA model belongs to parametric modeling—models that are fitted by known parameters. Normally, we classify this type of model as a statistical model because we need to make assumptions about what the data looks like. This is considerably different for wider machine learning models that do not have any preset assumptions about what the data looks like.

However, in a real banking scenario, a statistical approach is still prevalent among the econometrics, quantitative finance, and risk management domains. This approach works when we have a handful of data points, for example, around 30 to 100 data points. However, when we have a wealth of data, this approach may not fare as well as other machine learning approaches.

ARIMA assumes that there is a stationary trend that we can describe. The autoregressive terms, *p* and *d*, are each significant in their own way:

- *p* means the number of past period(s) that is affecting the current period value (for example, *p = 1: Y current period = Y current -1 period * coefficient + constant*).
- Non-seasonal difference (*d*) refers to the number of past periods progression impacting the current period values (for example, *d = 1*: the difference between *Y* now versus *Y* in the past period).
- Lagged terms (*q*) means the number of the past period's forecast errors impacting the current period values.

Consider an example in which *q = 1: Y* impacted by an error in the *t - 1* period—here, error refers to the difference between the actual and predicted values.

In a nutshell, ARIMA specifies how the previous period's coefficient, constant, error terms, and even predicted values impact the current predicted values. It sounds scary, but it is, in fact, very understandable.

After the model is fit, it will be asked to make a prediction and be compared against the actual testing data. The deviation of the prediction from the testing data will record the accuracy of the model. We will use a metric called the **Mean Square Error** (**MSE**) in this chapter to determine the fitness of the model to the data.

Introducing neural networks – the secret sauce for accurately predicting demand

We may have a good data source, but we should not forget that we also need a smart algorithm. You may have read about neural networks thousands of times, but let's look at a short explanation before we use them extensively throughout the book. A neural network is an attempt by a computer to mimic how our brain works—it works by connecting different computing points/neurons with different settings.

Architecture-wise, it looks like layers of formulas. Those of you reading this book probably have some background in algebra, and can see how the interested outcome Y is related to X, the variable, with b being the coefficient and c being the constant term:

$$Y = bX + c$$

Y is what we wish to predict on the left-hand side; on the right-hand side, $bX + c$ are the forms that describe how the feature (X) is related to Y. In other words, Y is the output, while X is the input. The neural network describes the relationship between the input and the output.

Suppose that Z is what we want to predict:

$$Z = dY + e$$

It seems that the formulas are linked:

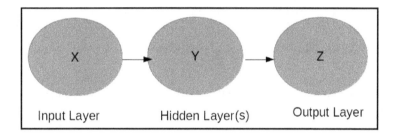

This is the simplest form of a neural network, with one input layer, one hidden layer, and one output layer. Each of the layers has one neuron (point).

I encourage you to read research papers and introductory text on machine learning or even enroll yourself for online courses. Useful resources from Packt include Sebastian Raschka and Vahid Mirjalili's *Python Machine Learning* (https://www.packtpub.com/big-data-and-business-intelligence/python-machine-learning-second-edition) and Rowel Atienza's *Advanced Deep Learning with Keras* (https://www.packtpub.com/big-data-and-business-intelligence/advanced-deep-learning-keras).

Backpropagation

There are other concepts in neural networks, such as backpropagation. This refers to the feedback mechanism that fine-tunes the neural network's parameters, which mostly connect neurons within the network (except when it is a constant parameter at the layer). It works by comparing the output at output layer Z (predicted) versus the actual value of Z (actual). The wider the gap between actual and predicted, the more adjustment of b, c, d, and e is needed.

Understanding how gaps are measured is also an important piece of knowledge—this is called **metrics** and will be addressed in `Chapter 3`, *Using Features and Reinforcement Learning to Automate Bank Financing*.

Neural network architecture

Architecture concerns the layers and number of neurons at each layer, as well as how the neurons are interconnected in a neural network. The input layer is represented as **features**. The output layer can be a single number or a series of numbers (called a **vector**), which generates a number ranging from 0 to 1 or a continuous value—subject to the problem domain.

For example, to understand the structure of a neural network, we can project that it will look like the following screenshot from TensorFlow Playground (`https://playground. tensorflow.org/`), which is the visualization of another network with the same hidden layers—three layers with a size of 6:

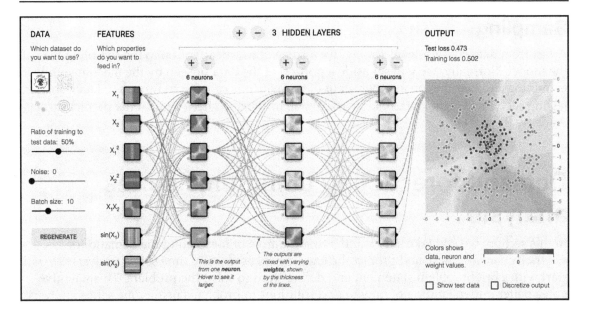

Using epochs for neural network training

Besides the design of the neural network, we also utilize the `epoch` parameter, which indicates the number of times the same set of data is fed to the neural network.

We need to increase the number of epochs if we do not have enough data to satisfy the number of parameters in neural networks. Given that we have X parameters in the neural network, we need at least X data points to be fed to the network. Unfortunately, if our data point is only $X/2$, we need to set `epoch` to 2 in order to make sure that we can feed X data points (all of them are fed twice) to the network.

Scaling

Before feeding the features to the machine learning model, we will normalize the input features of different magnitudes to be of the same magnitude. For example, the price and volume of goods are different types of numeric data. The scaling process will make sure that both of them are scaled to the same range, from 0 to 1. In classical statistical modeling processes, this step is very important to avoid a particular feature of bigger scales that dominate the influence on the prediction.

Sampling

Apart from data column-level scaling, we also need to pay attention to the sampling bias of the model. Normally, we will set aside a portion of the data unseen by the machine while it is training and learning on another set of data—which is called a **training set**. Later on, the testing set (which is the dataset kept aside) will be used to check against the prediction made by the model.

Demand forecasting using time series analysis

In this section, we will take a look at the first example of forecasting the demand for electricity consumption, and predict the energy expenses using time series analysis. We will start with a brief problem statement and define steps to solve the problem. This will give you a better understanding of how to find solutions to problems using time series analysis.

Today, electricity or energy is a very basic necessity for all of us. We use electricity and pay bills. Now, as a customer, we want to analyze electricity consumption and predict future consumption and predict energy expenses. This is the problem that we will solve in this section.

Time series analysis is the optimal approach for solving problems similar to the one defined in the preceding problem statement. Machine learning models need large datasets to be fed before the actual solution is derived. These large datasets are used by machine learning models to derive a pattern or identify an existing pattern that might not be visible when the data is scattered. Similarly, our first step would be to obtain a large amount of data and process it to extract meaningful information. This is going to be a three-step process. Here are the steps that we will follow:

1. Downloading the data
2. Preprocessing the data
3. Model fitting the data

Downloading the data

Start by downloading data regarding electricity consumption and energy expenses. Even though we can download data from public websites now, in a true production environment, it is not uncommon to download data from an internal database and pass it to users as a flat file (a text file with no database structure).

You can download the files from the following paths:

- **Consumption**: `https://www.eia.gov/opendata/qb.php?category=873sdid=ELEC.CONS_TOT.NG-CA-98.M`

- **Cost**: `https://www.eia.gov/opendata/qb.php?category=41625sdid=ELEC.COST.NG-CA-98.M`

- **Revenue**: `https://www.eia.gov/opendata/qb.php?category=1007sdid=E LEC.REV.CA-RES.M`

There are many ways of obtaining data, for example, using an API or robots. We will address these other methods of extracting data as we move further into the book. In `Chapter 4`, *Mechanizing Capital Market Decisions*, we'll obtain data through an API call. If we were to use a robot, for example, we could have used **Beautiful Soup** to parse the website or register the API. However, in this example, we simply visit the site using a browser and navigate to the download button to download the data.

Preprocessing the data

After we obtain the data, we align it together in the same time series, as the data we've downloaded can cover different periods of time. As data scientists, we strive to align our data in one single sheet of data, with all of the required data listed column by column (that is, cost, consumption, sales, and more):

A	B
Average cost of fossil fuels	for electricity generation coal California electric power (to
https://www.eia.gov/opendata/qb.php?category=41619&sdid=ELEC.COST.COW-CA-9	
08:07:14 GMT+0800 (HKT)	
Source: U.S. Energy Information Administration	
Month	Series ID: ELEC.COST.COW-CA-98.M dollars per tons
Jan 2018	0
Dec 2017	0
Nov 2017	0
Oct 2017	0
Sep 2017	0
Aug 2017	0
Jul 2017	0
Jun 2017	0
May 2017	0
Apr 2017	0
Mar 2017	0
Feb 2017	0
Jan 2017	0

Each line (or row) of the data should represent a single month. Right before we feed our data for the machine to learn the patterns, we will need to set aside some data for testing and some for learning. With the testing data, we can see whether the model predicts well, without training on the learning data first. This is a fundamental step in all ML/predictive models. We do not feed the testing dataset for ML/training. The line that calls the function is as follows:

```
file_path_out
if select_fld:
    list_flds = ['consumption_ng','avg_cost_ng']
    tuple_shape_list = [(8,0,3),(12,1,3)]
else:
    list_flds = preprocess_data(f_name,list_flds)
```

In this program, we set aside the earliest 70% of data points as training data for the machine to learn and adapt to, while keeping the latter 30% of data points as testing data. This is data that will be used to compare against the prediction made by the model, not used to fit the data.

Model fitting the data

Once the data is clean, we will start training the machine to learn about the pattern. The training data will be fed to the machine as fitting. The model is like a shirt and the training data is like the body we're attempting to fit it to.

Here are the steps to fit our data into an ARIMA model:

1. For each data file/field in the consolidated file, we run *step 3* and *step 4* (which have been marked in the code file for the following code block).
2. If the Boolean variable, parameter_op, is set to True, then we will run *step 5* (which is marked as well). This explores all the possible combinations of parameters in ARIMA with regard to p, d, and q, which are set as follows:

    - p: Ranging from 0 to 12
    - d: Ranging from 0 to 2
    - q: Ranging from 0 to 3

3. For combinations of any of the preceding values, we calculate the fitness of the data to the actual pattern and measure the error values. The combinations with the lowest error values are selected as the chosen parameters of the ARIMA model.

The following is the code snippet to fine-tune the parameters used (please refer to the full code file on GitHub: https://github.com/PacktPublishing/Hands-On-Artificial-Intelligence-for-Banking):

```
start = time.time()
lowest_MSE=99999999999
lowest_order = (0,0,0)
for p_para in range(13):
  for d_para in range(3):
    for q_para in range(4):
      order = (p_para,d_para,q_para)
      ...
      ...
      error,temp_data,temp_model = forecasting(dta_df, fld, False, \
                                               order, 0.7, fld)

if error<lowest_MSE:
  lowest_MSE=error
  lowest_order = order
  lowest_data = temp_data
  lowest_model = temp_model
  end = time.time()
  ...
```

Congratulations! We have now delivered a model that can provide volume forecasts for the future!

Procuring commodities using neural networks on Keras

In this section, we will take a look at another more complex example. As before, we will define the problem statement and then define steps to solve the problem.

In this example, we want to forecast the procurement of commodities based on historical data. The commodity that we are going to use is natural gas. In the case of natural gas, we do not have any control over its pricing because it is a hugely globalized commodity. However, we can still set up the internal procurement strategy when the pricing of the natural gas hits a certain range. The profitability ratio target will constrain the maximum pricing we can pay for the raw material to be profitable for the owners of the firm. We will track the profitability ratio, which is the ratio of cost of natural gas to sales.

Let's understand this pricing constraint with an example. In this example, we assume that for each dollar spent where the unit cost of natural gas (for electric power) increased, the cost of materials to sales of the energy company will increase by **9.18%** (this is based on 3 years of data):

DUKE ENERGY CORPORATION			
CONSOLIDATED STATEMENTS OF OPERATIONS			
		Years Ended December 31,	
(in millions, except per share amounts)	2017	2016	2015
Operating Revenues			
Regulated electric	$21,177	$21,221	$21,379
Regulated natural gas	1,734	863	536
Nonregulated electric and other	654	659	456
Total operating revenues	23,565	22,743	22,371
Operating Expenses			
Fuel used in electric generation and purchased power	6,350	6,625	7,355
Cost of natural gas	632	265	141
Operation, maintenance and other	5,788	6,085	5,539
Depreciation and amortization	3,527	3,294	3,053
Property and other taxes	1,233	1,142	1,129
Impairment charges	282	18	106
Total operating expenses	17,812	17,429	17,323

The following table shows the weighted average for sales on an annual basis:

	2017	2016	2015	Source
(i) Sales of regulated natural gas	1734	863	536	Duke Energy
(ii) Cost of natural gas	632	265	141	Duke Energy
(iii) = (ii)/(i) Cost of natural gas to sales	36.45%	30.71%	26.31%	calculated
(iv) Unit Weight Avg Mth Unit cost ($million/mcf)	3.91	3.18	3.44	US EIA – California
(v) = (iii) / (iv) conversion of Unit Cost to Cost of Materials rat	9.32%	9.66%	7.66%	calculated
(vi) = Weighted average of v by (i)	9.18%	9.18%	9.18%	calculated

Here, you can see the cost of natural gas to sales from **2015** to **2017**. In **2017**, at an average unit weight of **$3.91**, the cost of natural gas to sales is at **36.45%**. We assume that the average unit weight and cost to sales are in a constant relationship—averaging the values of the cost of materials rate across the years (from **2015-2017**, that is, **7.66%**, **9.32%**, and **9.66%**). We took an average of all three figures to come to a weighted average of **9.18%**.

Remember, the actual number should, in practice, come from the internal accounting system, not the external US **Energy Information Administration** (**EIA**) data that is used only for the purpose of electric power.

Based on the last 3 years of data, we find that the average cost of materials to sales stood at 31.15% (the average of **iii** from the table), which translates into $3.39 million/thousand cubic feet. The cost of the material of sales is at 36.24% with the unit cost at $3.95 million/mcf in the upper range. The **mcf** is a standard unit cost of natural gas. It is equal to a thousand cubic feet. However, at the lower range, the cost of the material of sales is 26.07% with the unit cost at $2.84 million/mcf. The unit conversion details can be found on the EIA website.

Data is extracted from the preceding sales figure table: *Operating Expenses/Operating Revenues = cost of materials to sales.*

After we have established the procurement plan, we then need to understand where to source the natural gas from. In real life, we would consider how the model's insight gets executed; perhaps we also need to build a model to make the subsequent decision on how the model's insights get executed. This is exactly what we have mentioned in business understanding on how to execute the order in exchange markets.

To complete this story, we assume that we purchase the natural gas from the exchange markets using physical deliveries whenever the price hits the target range for the quantity we forecasted.

Data flow

The following data flow outlines the steps we need to take in order to prepare and generate the code to build the commodity procurement model. The first box denotes a script run on the SQLite database; the other boxes denote steps run on Python:

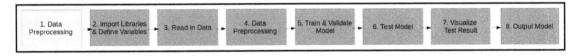

It generally fits into the framework of CRISP-DM, with different areas of focus throughout this book—some may focus on understanding the business, while some may focus on evaluation. The steps in the preceding diagram are covered in detail in the following sections.

Preprocessing the data (in the SQL database)

Data preprocessing means converting the data into the desired data features. We run it outside of Python coding to reduce the layers involved (that is, we interact directly with SQLite rather than using Python to interact with SQLite). Here are the steps involved in performing database operations:

1. Create the SQLite database.
2. Import the data as a staging table.
3. Create the required table(s)—a one-time operation.
4. Insert the staging table into the actual table with data type and format transformation.
5. Create the view that does the feature engineering.
6. Output the preprocessed view as CSV data.

Importing libraries and defining variables

Import libraries and define variables to make sure that the relevant functions can be used. Import all of the relevant libraries:

- `pandas`: This is for data storage before data is fed to the machine learning module.
- `keras`: This an easy-to-use machine learning framework that has another library.
- `tensorflow`: This is used as the backend.
- `sklearn`: This is a very popular machine learning module that provides lots of data preprocessing toolkits along with some machine learning models that are easy to use. The models are not used in this example, as we wish to build up the foundation for the more extensive use of machine learning models afterward. In addition, `sklearn` also has metrics that appraise the performance of the models.
- `matplotlib`: This is the default data visualization tool.

The following code block is the code importing all the listed libraries:

```
''' *****************************************
2. import all the libraries required
'''
import pandas as pd

from keras.models import Model
from keras.layers import Dense, Input
from sklearn.preprocessing import StandardScaler
```

```
from sklearn.model_selection import train_test_split
from sklearn.metrics import mean_squared_error

import matplotlib.pyplot as plt

import pickle

demand_model_path = 'demand_model.h5'
f_in_name = 'consumption_ng_exp.csv'
```

Reading in data

The following is the code snippet to read in the data and take on the result generated from *step 1*:

```
'''**************************************
#Read in data
'''
pd_trade_history = pd.read_csv(f_in_name,header=0)
pd_trade_history = pd_trade_history.drop('date_d',1)
```

Preprocessing the data (in Python)

Now we come to data preprocessing in Python. Some studies claim that data scientists spend 80% of their time on this step! It includes selecting features and target variables, checking/validating data types and handling missing values (this component is not included in this example to reduce complexity), and splitting data into a training set and a testing set. In some cases, when the ratios of the various classes of targets are not similar in quantity, we may need to do stratified sampling to ensure that balanced training samples are fed for machine learning. In this example, we set aside 20% for testing and 80% for training:

```
'''**************************************
4. Pre-processing data
'''
#4.A: select features and target
df_X = pd_trade_history.iloc[:,:-5]
df_Y = pd_trade_history.iloc[:,-4:]

np_X = df_X.values
np_Y = df_Y.values

#4.B: Prepare training and testing set
X_train, X_test, Y_train, Y_test = train_test_split(np_X, np_Y, \
```

```
                                           test_size = 0.2)

#4.C: scaling the inputted features
sc_X = StandardScaler()
X_train_t = sc_X.fit_transform(X_train)
X_test_t = sc_X.fit_transform(X_test)
```

Training and validating the model

We train the neural network by feeding the training dataset to generate a model. The following code snippet defines the machine learning model in Keras and trains it. It builds the deep neural network model with 329 parameters:

```
'''*************************************
#5. Build the model
'''
inputs = Input(shape=(14,))
x = Dense(7, activation='relu')(inputs)
x = Dense(7, activation='relu')(x)
x = Dense(7, activation='relu')(x)
x = Dense(4, activation='relu')(x)
x = Dense(4, activation='relu')(x)
x = Dense(4, activation='relu')(x)
x = Dense(4, activation='relu')(x)
predictions = Dense(units=4, activation='linear')(x)
demand_model= Model(inputs=inputs,outputs=predictions)
demand_model.compile(loss='mse', optimizer='adam', metrics=['mae'])

demand_model.fit(X_train_t,Y_train, epochs=7000, validation_split=0.2)

Y_pred = demand_model.predict(X_test_t)

#conver numpy as dataframe for visualization
pd_Y_test = pd.DataFrame(Y_test)
pd_Y_pred = pd.DataFrame(Y_pred)
```

Testing the model

We will compare the data points set aside (20%) in *step 4* against the predicted outcome based on the models trained and the features data:

```
'''****************************************
##6. Test model: Measure the model accuracy
combine both actual and prediction of test data into data
'''
data = pd.concat([pd_Y_test,pd_Y_pred], axis=1)
data_name = list(data)[0]
data.columns=['actual1','actual2','actual3','actual4','predicted1', \
              'predicted2','predicted3','predicted4']

error1 = mean_squared_error(data['actual1'],data['predicted1'])
print('Test MSE 1: %.3f' % error1)
error2 = mean_squared_error(data['actual2'],data['predicted2'])
print('Test MSE 1: %.3f' % error2)
error3 = mean_squared_error(data['actual3'],data['predicted3'])
print('Test MSE 1: %.3f' % error3)
error4 = mean_squared_error(data['actual4'],data['predicted4'])
```

Visualizing the test result

This step allows us to cross-check the metrics that represent the performance of the model—the MSE:

```
'''****************************************
#7. Visualize the prediction accuracy
'''

data.actual1.plot(color='blue',grid=True,label='actual1',title=data_name)
data.predicted1.plot(color='red',grid=True,label='predicted1')
plt.legend()
plt.show()
plt.close()

...
```

This will result in the following plot:

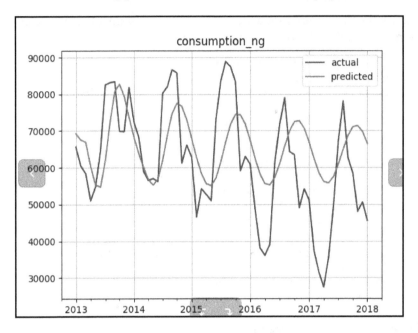

Generating the model for production

The model that was trained and tested in *steps 5* and *6* will be output as a file for the production system to run on unseen production data. We will output two files—one for scaling the input features and another one for the neural network:

```
'''**************************************
#8. Output the models
'''
demand_model.summary()
demand_model.save(demand_model_path)
f_scaler=open('x_scaler.pkl',"wb+")
pickle.dump(sc_X, f_scaler)
```

Congratulations! We have now delivered a model that can be used at the operational level to identify the quantity to order for this month's demand, next month, and the month after. The following diagram shows the steps in the training versus the deployment of machine learning models:

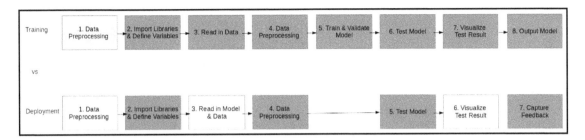

However, we are not going to cover deployment right now. We will keep this in mind and address the topic as we progress in this book. We will explore wrapping the AI production solution as an API in `Chapter 8`, *Building Personal Wealth Advisers with Bank APIs.*

Summary

In this chapter, you learned about time series analysis, M2M communication, and the benefits of time series analysis for commercial banking. We also looked at two useful examples by defining the problem statement and deriving the solution step by step. We also learned about the basic concepts of time series analysis and a few techniques, such as ARIMA.

In the next chapter, we will explore reinforcement learning. Reinforcement learning is an area of machine learning involving algorithms. The application takes an appropriate action to maximize the effectiveness of the outcome in a particular situation. We will also look at how to automate decision-making in banking using reinforcement learning. Exciting, isn't it?

3
Using Features and Reinforcement Learning to Automate Bank Financing

Commercial banks make money by earning interest on money that was loaned to borrowers. In many cases, the loan becomes a **Non-Performing Asset** (**NPA**) for the bank. There are instances where the borrower could go bankrupt, leaving the bank with a loss. In such situations, it becomes critical for commercial banks to assess the borrower's ability to repay the loan in a timely manner.

Now, if we look at this scenario closely, we realize that every loan is funded by the money deposited by other customers. Thus, the commercial bank owes interest to the depositor for the money deposited for a time period. This is usually the interest on the depositor's money that is credited by the banks on a quarterly basis. The bank also profits if it charges the borrower more interest and pays a low interest to the depositor.

In this chapter, we will derive the solution for both of these situations by using **Reinforcement Learning** (**RL**), which is an important area of machine learning. Apart from this, we shall also look at examples of how RL can be helpful in banking functions. RL is one of the three areas of machine learning, with the others being supervised learning and unsupervised learning. RL is specifically applicable where decision-making is required based on the surroundings or the current environment. In RL, an agent is presented with options to move toward the reward. The agent has to choose one of the options available. If the correct option is chosen, the agent gets a reward. Otherwise, the agent gets penalized. The goal for the agent is to maximize their chance of getting closer to the reward with each step and to ultimately obtain it.

All of these concepts shall be divided into the following topics:

- Breaking down the functions of a bank
- AI modeling techniques
- Metrics of model performance
- Building a bankruptcy prediction model
- Funding the loan using reinforcement learning

Before we move forward and learn about RL, it is necessary to understand the banking business and how it functions.

Breaking down the functions of a bank

Within a bank, as an intermediary between those with excess money (the depositors) and those who need money (the borrowers), there are two important questions that need to be answered:

- How risky is a borrower?
- What is the funding cost of money?

These are the two important questions that need to be considered before we look at the profit required for sustaining the business operations in order to cover its running costs.

When these decisions are not made properly, it threatens the viability of a bank. There could be two possible outcomes in such instances:

- If the bank does not make enough profit to cover the cost of risk and operations when a risky event occurs, the bank could collapse.
- If the bank fails to meet the depositor's requirements or fails to honor its borrower's agreements to lend, it hurts the credibility of the bank, thus driving potential customers away.

Major risk types

To answer the question, *How risky is a borrower?*, we first need to understand the factors contributing to risk.

Risk is an unfavorable outcome in the future that impacts the functioning of a bank. For a bank, the major contributors include the following:

- **Credit risk**: This risk concerns the borrower's inability to repay the capital back to the bank in a lending transaction; for example, the financial distress of the borrowing firm, causing its inability to repay the loan.
- **Market risk**: This risk concerns unfavorable price movements in financial markets, such as an interest rate hike in the market from which the bank sources its funding.
- **Operational risk**: This risk concerns events happening in the operations of the bank as an organization. This could include internal theft, a cyber attack, and so on.

For a complete list of the types of risk, please refer to the Basel Framework by BIS (`https://www.bis.org/bcbs/basel3.htm`).

Asset liability management

Commercial banks need deposits in order to fund loans. As well as assessing the riskiness of borrowers, the bank also performs a useful function in that they convert deposits from savers into loans for borrowers. Thus, a pricing mechanism for both depositors and borrowers is important. To a bank, loans sit on the asset side of financial statements, while deposits sit on the liabilities side of the business. Therefore, this is often called **Asset and Liability Management** (**ALM**).

In this book, we will focus on only one part of the entire ALM function – the funding aspect – without covering other risks such as liquidity risk, interest rate risk, and foreign exchange risk. The following are the objectives of the ALM function of a bank:

- The first objective of ALM is to ensure that loans are supported by deposits and that the bank will have sufficient deposits, in case the depositors ask for their money back. In terms of the total quantity, approximately, a $100 deposit supports a $70 loan. Referencing the ratios from some of the biggest banks, the ratios should be around 1.2:1 to 1.5:1 for a customer deposit to a customer loan.

- Secondly, there is another aspect with regard to how long deposits are placed for and loans are lent out. The question of how long is referred to as the **duration**. To meet long-term loan commitments, the bank also needs deposits to be locked in for a long enough time to ensure that loans are supported by deposits in a long-term manner.

- Thirdly, the ALM function needs to be profitable, which means the ALM income should be higher than the ALM cost. The *cost* is the ALM pricing that you are giving out. This cost is, in fact, the income for ALMs/banks, while the deposit rate quoted to the client is the bank's expense.

Part of a bank's well-known secret for profit is to convert the short-term deposit (lower-priced) into a long-term loan (higher interest income). The following curve shows the pricing aspect for a bank for its deposits and loans:

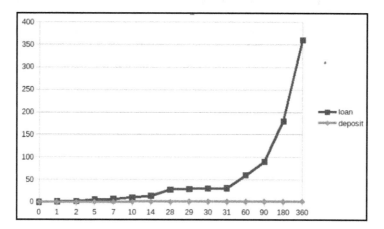

In the preceding graph, the *x* axis shows how long (in days) the deposit/loan position will remain with the bank, while the *y* axis shows the annualized interest rate.

Interest rate calculation

Though there are many ways to calculate the interest to be paid on the deposit, the most common way to calculate interest is to quote the interest in its annualized form; that is, as if the interest has been put in place for a year, regardless of how long it will be placed for.

For example, if the 7-day interest rate for a deposit is 1%, this means that within 7 days, we will get the following:

$$(1 + \frac{1}{365}) \times \frac{7}{365} = 1 + i$$

We only need to divide the annualized interest rate by 7 days in order to get what we shall get for the 7-day period. The reason behind this is that it is useful for a market dealer to have a standardized way to quote pricing.

We will use this formula for interest pricing and deposit pricing in the *Funding a loan using reinforcement learning* section, later in this chapter. However, there are a lot of other fine details with regard to interest pricing, with different ways of compounding (interest can be earned from interest) and day-count conventions (365 days, actual calendar or actual working days, 360 days, 220 days, and so on). For illustration purposes, we will assume a year is made up of 365 days and we will use simple interest rates without compounding.

Credit rating

Besides the cost of lending described in ALM, another role of the bank is to assess the level of risk when getting involved with a client. This riskiness is added to the cost of funding. This concept is known as **credit rating** in banks.

The Basel Committee assesses and imposes global regulations on risk management in banks. According to the definition provided by the *Definition on Default/Loss* by the Basel Committee (`https://www.bis.org/bcbs/qis/qis3qa_f.htm`), credit rating predicts the probability of a borrower (who is the one being rated) going bankrupt in a year's time. Borrowers usually default on a loan due to the bankruptcy of companies. So, we normally use default and bankruptcy interchangeably.

The essential question is, given the required information, how likely is it that the company could go bankrupt within 1 year, thus failing to meet its repayment obligation? This could be driven by many reasons, but one obvious reason is that the financial health of the company is not good.

A financial statement is like the report card of a company – even though it takes time to produce, it conforms to a certain internationally accepted standard and comes with the guarantee of quality by the auditors.

AI modeling techniques

Now that we've understood the functions of a business, it's time to move onto some technical concepts. In this section, we will learn about AI modeling techniques, including Monte Carlo simulation, the logistic regression model, decision trees, and neural networks.

Monte Carlo simulation

Monte Carlo simulation uses heavy computation to predict the behavior of objects by assuming random movements that can be described by probability. This approach is a standard tool that's used to study the movements of molecules in physics, which can only be predicted with a certainty of the movement pattern, which is described by probability.

Finance professionals adopt this method to describe the pricing movement of securities. We will use it to simulate pricing in the *Funding the loan using reinforcement learning* section, later in this chapter.

The logistic regression model

The logistic regression model is one of the most popular adoptions of AI in banking, especially in the domain of credit risk modeling. The target variable of the model will be a binary outcome of 1 or 0, with a probability of meeting the target of 1. The decision of what 1 and 0 refer to depends on how we prepare the data.

In this case, the target variable can be a company filing for bankruptcy within 1 year. The model is called logistic because the function that models the 1 and 0 is called **logit**. It is called regression because it belongs to a statistical model called the regression model, which strives to determine the causation of factors of an outcome.

Decision trees

The decision tree algorithm actually belongs to the supervised learning group of algorithms. However, due to the nature of the algorithm, it is commonly used to solve regression and classification problems. Regression and classification often require decision-making based on the situation at hand. So, these problems are commonly solved using reinforcement learning algorithms.

The beneficial element of having a decision tree is that we can actually visualize the decision tree's representation. The decision-making process starts at the top of the tree and branches out toward the leaf nodes of the tree. The leaf nodes are the point at which the target variables will end up. All the values of a variable that are classified to the same leaf node contain the same probability of defaulting. The following is an example visualization of a decision tree algorithm that is making a decision to give a loan to the applicant:

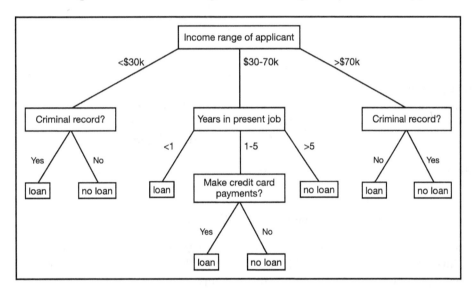

The most common way to move forward in the decision tree is to look at the minimal leaf size, which refers to the size of the bucket that each of the training samples is being classified in. If the bucket contains too few samples than `min_samples_leaf` dictates, then it will be scrapped. This can be done to reduce the number of buckets (known as the **leaf node of a decision tree**).

Reading the decision tree is easy. However, it is quite amazing to realize how the machine learns about the various conditions used for splitting.

Neural networks

A simple neural network looks like the one shown in the following diagram:

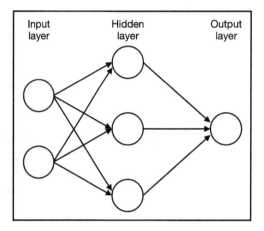

It consists of three layers, namely the **input layer**, the **hidden layer**, and the **output layer**. Each layer is made up of nodes. The artificial neural network that is used to solve AI problems mimics the physical neural network present in the human brain. The neurons in the human brain are represented by nodes in the artificial neural network. The connections between the neurons are represented in the artificial neural network by weights.

Let's understand the significance of each of the layers in the neural network. The input layer is used to feed the input into the model. It is also responsible for presenting the condition that the model is being trained for. Every neuron or node in the input layer represents one independent variable that has influence over the output.

The hidden layer is the most crucial because its job is to process the data it has received from the input layer and is responsible for extracting the necessary features from the input data. The hidden layer consists of one or more layers.

In the case of solving a problem with linearly represented data, the activation function (which processes the input data) can be included in the input layer itself. However, for processing complex representations of data, one or more hidden layers are required. The number of hidden layers depends on the complexity of the data. The hidden layer passes on the processed data to the output layer.

The output layer is responsible for collecting and transmitting information. The pattern that the output layer presents can be traced back to the input layer. The number of nodes in the output layer depends on the number of decisions to be made eventually.

Reinforcement learning

In the case of reinforcement learning, the model receives feedback on every step that it takes. First, let's understand the entities involved in reinforcement learning:

- **Agent**: This is someone who acts; in our case, it is the bank.
- **Actions**: This is the actual work done by the agent. In our case, actions refer to the pricing grid offered by the bank.
- **Utility function**: This assigns numbers to represent the desirability of a state. The utility function is learned via interactions from the feedback given by the actual **Profit and Loss** (**P&L**)/funding status versus pricing grids (both deposit and loan) offered.
- **Rewards**: This is the numeric representation of the desirability of the outcome. In our case, it is cumulative P&L (the binary result of meeting or failing the self-funding target, with 1 representing meeting and 0 representing failing). The cumulative P&L will equal 0 if the bank fails the self-funding requirements.
- **Policy**: Choose the action based on the utilities estimated. In our case, our policy does not evolve as it strives to take the pricing grid that provides the maximum next states' rewards. The policy we have leads to exploitation, not exploration, which means the policy does not give away current P&L to generate long-term P&L. This is because the depositors and borrowers will display a certain level of stickiness if they witness non-profitability in the short term while gaining P&L over the long term. Exploration is a normal action among relationship bankers, who treasure the long-term profitability of relationships.

Deep learning

With each of the models or techniques that we are learning, the complexity increases. In this example, we will assume that there will be 36 variables/features in the input layer. There will be two variables/features in the output layer – one for profitability and one for the self-funding status. There will be two hidden layers in-between the input and output layers – one next to the input layer with 10 neurons, followed by another layer with 15 neurons. This example will form a neural network that makes general pricing decisions for banks.

To estimate the profitability and self-funding status of the neural network, there are 127 variables in the input layer, three hidden layers each with 15 neurons, and one output layer with one output neuron to generate profitability (cumulative profit and loss for the day) or the percentage of client deposit to client loan.

In comparison to the logistic regression model, the input features are much more complex in the case of deep learning and the number of parameters involved is in the magnitude of 10 times more or above.

The following table shows a summary of the pricing model:

Layer	Shape	No of parameters
Input	(1, 36)	0
Hidden 1	(1, 10)	370
Hidden 2	(1, 15)	165
Hidden 3	(1, 15)	240
Total parameters		775

In the preceding table, the first column lists which layer it is – input or hidden. The second column represents the shape of the layer in terms of the number of parameters connected from the previous layer to the current layer.

To calculate the number of parameters, let's consider the **Hidden 1** layer. In this case, 36 features from the previous layer connect to 10 neurons in the current layer. We also need constants equal to the number of features in the current layer to achieve scaling across features. So, the total parameters come to 36*10 + 10 = 370 parameters in the **Hidden 1** layer.

Knowing how to count the parameters helps us see whether the amount of training data is sufficient enough to train the network. It is strongly suggested that we ensure that the number of parameters is at least equal to *number of records * number of epochs*. Think of how many formulas will be required to determine a problem with two variables – at least two. The formula is like training data in deep learning, while the variables are like the parameters of the network.

Metrics of model performance

When we build an AI model, the most important aspect of the process is to define a way to measure the performance of a model. This enables the data scientist to decide how to improve and pick the best model.

In this section, we will learn about three common metrics that are commonly used in the industry to assess the performance of the AI model.

Metric 1 – ROC curve

The **Receiver Operating Characteristic** (**ROC**) metric measures how well the classifier performs its classification job versus a randomized classifier. The classifier that's used in this metric is a binary classifier. The binary classifier classifies the given set of data into two groups on the basis of a predefined classification rule.

This is linked to a situation where, say, we compare this model against flipping a fair coin to classify the company as being default or non-default, with heads indicating default and tails indicating non-default. Here, there's a 50% chance of classifying default and a 50% chance of classifying non-default.

For a completely randomized predictive system such as coin flipping, it is very likely that the probability of hitting a true positive is the same as hitting a false positive rate. But in the case of companies defaulting in 1 year, in the following example, it is 6.3% (123 out of 1,828), which means we have an actual count of 1,828 non-default cases and 123 default cases. A truly random model will predict half of the default cases as non-default.

Let's plot a chart that shows the true positive and false positive rate as an ROC chart. True or false means the prediction that was made for the default event is factually true or false. Positive means that the classifier is positive (equals 1, which is default, in this case).

When we make no prediction, the true positive and false positive rate is 0. When we have gone through 50% of the sample, which is given as 1,951/2, we should be getting 50% of the sample by default, where 50% of the guesses are false positive. When we get to 100% of the sample, we should have 100% of the sample as true positive and 100% as false positive.

This randomized classifier's performance is denoted by the dotted line in this diagram:

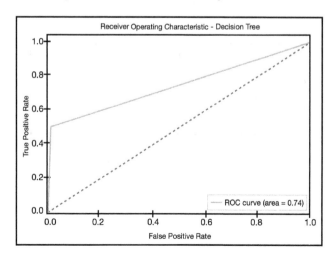

In the most ideal classifier case, we should be able to improve the true positive rate to 100%, with the false positive rate at 0% (denoted by the yellow line in the preceding diagram).

For the worst classifier, which classifies everything as 100% incorrect, the true positive rate should be 0% and the false positive rate should be 100% (denoted by the red dot). The use of ROC is also prevalent in credit risk model validation.

Metric 2 – confusion matrix

The confusion matrix is the most popular metric used to measure the performance of a classifier and has two outcomes:

		Actual: Ground Truth	
		True Default	False/Non-default
Prediction by Classifier	Positive/Default	62	27
	Negative/Non-default	61	1,801
		True Positive Rate = 62/(62+61)	False Positive Rate = 27/(27+1,801)

The confusion matrix also provides results similar to the ROC curve. The major idea behind this is to separate prediction and the ground truth by rows and columns.

Metric 3 – classification report

The classification report is another way to appraise the performance of the model, with the following indicators:

	precision	recall	f1-score	support
0	0.97	0.99	0.98	1828
1	0.69	0.50	0.58	123
avg / total	0.95	0.95	0.95	1951

The details of the indicators are as follows:

- **Precision and recall:** Precision addresses the true positive rate of the model prediction, while recall addresses the coverage of the model. Precision measures the percentage of the predicted value being the predicted value. Recall measures the percentage of the target values being predicted as the expected values.
- **F1-score**: One of the most important measures of the overall accuracy of the model is the F1-score. It is the harmonic mean of precision and recall. This is what we use to compare the performance of models.
- **Support**: This is another term that means the number of records that are of the value listed in the leftmost column. There are 123 actual default cases (with target *value = 1* under the *default* column).

Building a bankruptcy risk prediction model

The bank, as the lender, needs to dictate the interest rates that will cover the cost of lending. The bank provides the interest rate by considering its cost of borrowing from others, plus the risk that the company might file for bankruptcy after taking the loan from the bank.

In this example, we shall assume the role of a banker to assess the probability of the borrowers becoming bankrupt. The data for this has been obtained from data.world (`https://data.world`), which provides us with the data for the bankruptcy predictions for different companies. The data available at this link was collected from the **Emerging Markets Information Services** (**EMIS**). The EMIS database has information about the emerging markets in the world.

EMIS analyzed bankrupt companies for the period 2000-2012 and operating companies for the period 2007-2013. After the data was collected, five classifications were made based on the forecasting period. The first year class is the data that contains the financial rates from the year of the forecasting period. Another class label shows what the bankruptcy status would be after 5 years.

Obtaining the data

We are going to use an open source program for data conversion, followed by another program to train a model from the data downloaded:

1. We begin by obtaining the data that has been downloaded from a new data source. However, it is downloaded via a browser, and not via a data feed. Files ending with `.arff` will be obtained from data.world. The URL for this is `https://data.world/uci/polish-companies-bankruptcy-data`. Usually, we can use 1-year bankruptcy data as the model predicts bankruptcy within 1 year. For the sake of our example, we will use a dataset containing 5 years' worth of data.

2. We will then preprocess the data, as well as performing feature engineering by extraction, transformation, and loading. In this case, the file that will be downloaded from data.world is in `.arff` file format, which can't be read easily by Python. The code that can be used to convert the file type can be found on GitHub (`https://github.com/jeffreynghm/AIFinance_Packt`).

Building the model

In this example, we will try out three types of models: logistic regression, decision tree, and neural network.

Before the computing power becomes readily available, it is quite common to choose the model according to the problem we are trying to solve, as well as what answers we need from the machine. However, nowadays, we tend to try out all possible models and pick the best model that delivers the best performance.

In this case, we can label it as something we want to predict. The target behavior that we wish to predict is the company default—this is called a target variable in the machine learning world. We will establish how accurate the model is at predicting the target variable when given the input data by deploying common metrics to compare performance across different models.

In this example, we will need the following libraries:

- `os`: For file path manipulation.
- `re`: Regular expression for matching column headers.
- `pandas`: DataFrame to keep the data.
- `matplotlib.pyplot`: For plotting the model's result to showcase its accuracy.

- `seaborn`: A beautiful visualization tool for data analysis.
- `sklearn`: A machine learning library, including very strong data preparation for splitting, training, and testing sets, rescaling the data values to feed to the neural network, handling missing values or value abnormality, and so on.
- `pickle`: The file format that's used to save the model generated from the machine learning process.
- `graphviz`: Used to visualize the decision tree.

The steps are as follows:

1. Import all the relevant libraries using the following code:

```
import os
import re
import pandas as pd
import matplotlib.pyplot as plt
import seaborn as sns

from sklearn.metrics import classification_report,roc_curve,
auc,confusion_matrix,f1_score
from sklearn.model_selection import train_test_split
from sklearn.feature_selection import RFE
from sklearn import linear_model,tree
from sklearn.neural_network import MLPClassifier
from sklearn.preprocessing import StandardScaler

import pickle
import graphviz
```

For logistic regression, when it comes to deciding which features are to be chosen, we will rely on testing the accuracy of different features. The combination that delivers the highest accuracy will be chosen.

2. Define the `optimize_RFE()` function, which will perform the feature selection process. This function will try out different combinations of features that give the highest true positive and the lowest possible false positive. We will measure the performance in order to decide on the number of features that generate the best performance. The following is the code for the function definitions:

```
def select_columns(df, col_list):
    ...
def generate_column_lists(col_support,col_list):
    ...
def optimize_RFE(logreg, X, Y, target_features = 10):
    ...
```

```
        while trial_cnt<=target_features:
            rfe = RFE(logreg,trial_cnt,verbose=1)
            ...
            select_cols = generate_column_lists(col_support, col_list)
            X_selected = select_columns(X,select_cols)
            ...
            #build model
            ...
            ##metric 1: roc
            ...
            #memorize this setting if this ROC is the highest
            ...
        return max_roc_auc, best_col_list, result_list

    def train_logreg(X,Y):
        print('Logistic Regression')
        logreg = linear_model.LogisticRegression(C=1e5)
        roc_auc, best_col_list, result_list = optimize_RFE(logreg, \
                                                    X, Y, 20)
        scaler = StandardScaler()
        scaler.fit(X_train)
        ...
        ##metric 1: roc
        ...
        ##metric 2: Confusion matrix
        Y_pred_logreg = logreg.predict(X_test)
        confusion_matrix_logreg = confusion_matrix(Y_test, \
                                                    Y_pred_logreg)
        ...
        #common standard to compare across models
        f1_clf = f1_score(Y_test, Y_pred_logreg, average='binary')
        ##Quality Check: test for dependency
        ...
        ##save model
    ...
```

3. Besides a logic regression model, we will also build a decision tree. Feature selection will be performed by the algorithm at the time of training. Therefore, unlike the logistic regression model, we do not need to limit the number of features that are provided as input to the training process:

```
    '''
    ## Decision Tree
    '''
    #feed in data to the decision tree
    def train_tree(X,Y):
        print('Decision Tree')
        #split the dataset into training set and testing set
```

```
...
tree_clf = \
    tree.DecisionTreeClassifier(min_samples_leaf=min_leaf_size)

#preprocessing the data
scaler = StandardScaler()
scaler.fit(X_train)
...
#fit the training data to the model
...
##metric 1: roc
...
##metric 2: Confusion matrix
...
#common standard to compare across models
...
##save model
...
```

4. Lastly, we will add a neural network into the mix of models. It is similar to the decision tree. Feature selection will be performed by the algorithm at training time. However, it is important to perform a grid search for hyperparameter tuning. The hyperparameters that we are searching for belong to the neural network architecture; that is, how many layers we need to build to deliver the maximum performance. The following code is used to train the logistic regression model:

```
##Grid search that simulate the performance of different neural
network #design
def grid_search(X_train,X_test,
Y_train,Y_test,num_training_sample):
    ...
    #various depth
    for depth in range(1,5):
        ...
        for layer_size in range(1,8):
            ...
            nn_clf = MLPClassifier(alpha=1e-5, \
                    hidden_layer_sizes=hidden_layers_tuple, \
                    random_state=1)
            ...
    ...
    #various size

def train_NN(X,Y):
    print('Neural Network')
    #split the dataset into training set and testing set
```

```
...
#preprocessing the data
scaler = StandardScaler()
scaler.fit(X_train)
...
```

For all the models listed in this chapter, we also need to measure the accuracy. We are going to use two different approaches to measure accuracy. Various metrics are used in this classification problem. However, we need to be certain when it comes to building a machine learning model that classifies a company as default or non-default.

5. After defining these functions, we use the following code sample to actually call the function. All three models are built one by one. The results are stored in `f1_list` so that they can be printed out later:

```
f1_list = []
f1_score_temp= 0

#logistic regression model
log_reg,f1_score_temp = train_logreg(X,Y)
f1_list.append(f1_score_temp)
log_reg.get_params()

#decision tree
tree_clf,f1_score_temp = train_tree(X,Y)
f1_list.append(f1_score_temp)
tree_clf.get_params()

#neural network
nn_clf,f1_score_temp = train_NN(X,Y)
f1_list.append(f1_score_temp)
nn_clf.get_params()
```

6. Visualize the performance of each model using the following code:

```
'''
#4 Visualize the result
'''
print('*******************')
print('f1 of the models')
print(f1_list)
print('*******************')
```

7. Use the following code sample to visualize the model:

```
#for visualization of decision tree
x_feature_name = fields_list[:-1]
y_target_name = fields_list[-1]
d_tree_out_file = 'decision_tree'
dot_data = tree.export_graphviz(tree_clf, out_file=None,
                        feature_names=x_feature_name,
                        class_names=y_target_name,
                        filled=True, rounded=True,
                        special_characters=True)
graph = graphviz.Source(dot_data)
graph.render(d_tree_out_file)
```

In the next section, we will use reinforcement learning to decide whether the loan to the customer shall be funded or not.

Funding a loan using reinforcement learning

Assuming that our role is the head of the bank, it becomes important to figure out the cost of funding the loan. The problem we are solving is comprised of three parties (or as we call them, **agents**)—the bank, depositors, and borrowers. To begin with, we assume that there is only one bank but many depositors and borrowers. The depositors and borrowers will be created through randomized generated data.

When it comes to simulating different behaviors for these parties in machine learning, each of these is called an agent or an instance of an object. We need to create thousands of agents, with some being depositors, some being borrowers, one being a bank, and one being a market. These represent the collective behavior of competing banks. Next, we will describe the behavior of each type of agent.

Let's say we assume the role of treasurer of the bank or head of the treasury. The job of the head of the treasury is to quote the risk-free funding cost. The banker dealing with the customer will take the cost of funding and add the credit risk premium to make up the total cost of financing. Any extra margin higher than this total cost of financing shall be the net contribution of the banker. But when it comes to reporting on financial statements, actual interest income from the client will net off the net interest cost paid to by depositor or borrower to the bank.

What we want to produce is loan and deposit pricings for each maturity (1 day, 2 days, and so on) before the bank opens for business. There is no such dataset in the public domain. Therefore, we will simulate the data. Maturity, amount of loan or deposit, starting date, and interest rate will all be simulated.

Understanding the stakeholders

While defining the solution using AI modeling, we usually simulate the behavior of the entities involved. It becomes critical for us to understand the behavior of stakeholders first. For the sake of this example, we must understand the behavioral aspects of three entities – the bank, the depositor, and the borrower.

A bank has two objectives:

- Generate the pricing grid for the deposit and the loan.
- Calculate its profit/loss, as well as its self-funding status at any point in time.

The pricing grid for the deposit and the loan is assumed to be priced at a different maturity.

In this example, reinforcement learning has been introduced to update the pricing, as well as to take on feedback by considering the impact of recent actions on the profit and loss and asset and liability ratios. Depositors are assumed to have varying expectations for the deposit interest as and when the deposit matures. At the end of the day, we assume the depositor is claiming their own interest income, along with the amount of deposit reported in the bank's account.

During the day before the market opens and on the maturity date of the deposit, the depositor will consider whether they want to stay or withdraw the deposit. At this point, we simulate the decision by randomizing the decision by generating a % chance of expected interest. There is a 50% chance of expectation for interest increasing and a 50% demand for the interest reducing. This expectation will then be compared against the bank's offer rate at that specific maturity. If the bank meets this expectation, then the deposit will stay; otherwise, the deposit will leave the bank for the same maturity period.

With regard to how the interest rate expectation changes, there are two variations used for depositors: one is completely linear, while the other follows a normal distribution. If the deposit leaves the bank, we assume that the same amount of deposit will be placed in another bank. So, on the maturity date of the deposit in the other bank, the depositors will set their expectations and evaluate whether to stay or go back to the original bank.

For the borrower, the behavior is assumed to be the same as the depositors', with the same day-end accrual activities. However, during the day, borrowers whose loans mature on the same day will reconsider their intention to stay or not. This is represented by the interest rate expectation and the exact method of simulation is the same as depositors'—but with the difference that the loan offered by the bank has to be lower than the expected pricing of the borrowers for it to stay for refinancing.

Arriving at the solution

The following are the steps for creating the borrowers and depositors to close the bank's book on a daily basis:

1. First, we need to import the data from the list of loans and deposits to generate a list of borrowers and depositors. In this step, scenarios are loaded from a spreadsheet to simulate the borrowers and depositors that come in on different days. The following code sample shows the function definition for generating the list of borrowers and depositors:

```
##Step 1: Import Data from the list of Loans and Deposits
##Based on an input file, generate list of borrowers and depositors
at the beginning
##Keep the master copy of clean clients list
'''
list_depositors_template,list_borrowers_template =
generate_list(f_deposit_path,f_loan_path,start_date)
```

2. At the beginning of each iteration (except the first day of business), the market pricing is provided and the bank needs to provide pricing as well. We generate a fixed amount of simulation (1,000 times). In each simulation, we assume a period of 10 years (3,650 days = 365days/year x 10 years). On any given day, depositors and borrowers set their expectations by referencing the market rate. When we begin the first day of each simulation, depositors and borrowers are created from the list of deposits and loans. The following code runs 1,000 simulations:

```
print('running simulation')
for run in range(0,1000):
    print('simulation ' +str(run))
    #reward function reset
    reward = 0

    list_depositors = copy.deepcopy(list_depositors_template)
    list_borrowers = copy.deepcopy(list_borrowers_template)
    ...
```

Executing the preceding code will create an object of the bank. At that time, two neural networks are initialized inside the bank – one for the deposit pricing and one for the loan pricing. The same thing is done for the bank called **market**.

Market pricing is randomized based on the initial pricing input into the market by Monte Carlo simulation. Based on the market pricing, borrowers and depositors set their expectations by referencing the market pricing, along with the tendency to attribute. After setting their expectations, two variations of the deposit pricing and loan pricing grids are generated.

3. Deposit pricing and loan pricing are generated by two neural networks and Monte Carlo simulations. The neural network dictates the required grid movement for the loan and deposit pricing grids. However, the `bank` object also generates randomized pricing based on the pricing generated by the neural network. The following code is used to build the model:

```
#build a model if this is the first run, otherwise, load the saved
model
#bank and environment objects created
...
deposit_pricing_grid_pred =
jpm.generate_deposit_grid(deposit_constant_grid)
loan_pricing_grid_pred = jpm.generate_loan_grid(loan_constant_grid)
loan_pricing_grid_prev = loan_empty_grid
deposit_pricing_grid_prev = deposit_empty_grid
loan_pricing_grid_final = loan_empty_grid
deposit_pricing_grid_final = deposit_empty_grid

#market is also a bank (collective behavior of many banks)
#market object created
market = bank()
...

daily_loan_list=[]
daily_deposit_list=[]
daily_net_asset_list=[]
cum_income_earned =0
cum_expense_paid =0

mkt_expense = 0
mkt_income = 0

for i_depositor in list_depositors_template:
...

for i_borrower in list_borrowers_template:
...
```

With this, the environment has been created. Here, the environment object contains the neural network model that provides the reward estimation for the given pricing grids (loan and deposit), as well as external environments such as market pricing, maturing borrowers, and depositors.

4. Generate a pricing grid for the day:

```
##Generate two pricing grids for the day
mkt_deposit_pricing_grid, mkt_loan_pricing_grid = \
                          market.generate_pricing_grids_MC()
loan_pricing_grid_pred,x_np_loan = jpm.generate_loan_grid_ML(...)
deposit_pricing_grid_pred,x_np_deposit = \
                          jpm.generate_deposit_grid_ML(...)
loan_pricing_grid_prev = loan_pricing_grid_final
deposit_pricing_grid_prev = deposit_pricing_grid_final
...
```

The pricing model of the bank is based on the machine learning model. The market is based on the randomized process referencing the initial values we hardcoded. At the same time, the maturity profile (loan and deposit maturing today) will be calculated and the customers' expectation for pricing is established. This expectation is based on market pricing and the internal demand randomized by the helper function defined.

5. Generate the list of possible pricings, predict the reward, and pick the best pricing. This step is called **action** in the reinforcement learning domain. Action is the act of quoting prices to customers and market peers. Based on the pricing generated in the previous step, we create a lot more variations (20, in our case) with a randomized process:

```
## Generating list of all possible loan / deposit pricing,
including previous, and current predicted pricing
...
#generate lots of variations:
for i in range(0,num_randomized_grid):
...
#accessing each of the choice
...
## Predict the reward values of each the variation and make the
choice of pricing
for loan_i in range(0,num_grid_variations):
    for deposit_i in range(0,num_grid_variations):
        ...
    #Policy A
    if max_reward<= temp_reward:
        ...
```

```
#Policy B: if both conditions fail, randomize the choice
...
#Policy C: Choose the best choice & reward
...
```

Using the environment object's machine learning model, we can predict the outcome of each of the variations and choose the best variation to maximize the profitability, satisfying the funding requirements with the deposit.

6. Execute the pricing grid. Income and expenses are generated based on the chosen pricing grid that generates the maximum estimated net profit while meeting the self-funding balance objective. Once the bank's pricing grid has been chosen, it is executed with the maturing borrowers and depositors. Some will stay and some will leave the bank:

```
#Carry forward the deposit and Roll-over the loan
#stay or not
##Update borrower and depositor
for i_borrower in list_borrowers:
...
for i_depositor in list_depositors:
...

# Actualized p n l
##************************************
# with clients
for i_borrower in list_borrowers:
#pocket in the loan interest
...

for i_depositor in list_depositors:
#pay out the deposit interest
...
#market operations
...
##************************************
#End of day closing
##************************************
#cumulative income = income earned from client + income earned from
market (if any excess deposit placed overnight)
...

#cumulative expense = expense paid to the client + expense paid to
market (if any insufficient deposit to fund overnight pos)
...
#Closed book for the day
...
```

```
f_log.write('\n***************summary run:' +str(run) + ' day '
+str(day_cnt)+'***************')
. . .
```

At the end of the day, interest will be accrued for those who stay with the bank and will be updated in the bank's accounting book (variables in the `bank` object). The daily position is also output to the log file.

The winning combination will be fed to the model for further reinforcement learning both for the bank and the environment. The feedback will contain the actual P&L for the bank for both deposit and loan grid pricing; for the environment, the actual profitability and self-funding status will be fed back to the reward model.

The actual P&L and self-funding statuses are provided as feedback to the `environment` object and `bank` object in order to predict the reward and pricing more accurately.

7. After each simulation, the results are saved in an output file and we get to monitor the progress of reinforcement learning. At the end of each simulation, the last day's snapshot result is output. Use the following code to generate the output:

   ```
   #output result of this run and save model
   print('run ' + str(run) + ' is completed')
   . . .
   ```

Each bar on the *x* axis represents the average P&L of 10 simulations. The P&L of the simulation peaked at the eighth bar. By performing a detailed analysis of each simulation result in the log file, we can see that the improvement of P&L stopped at the eighty-seventh simulation since P&L plateaued and stabilized at the eightieth plus simulation. With further training, the P&L dropped, thus showing signs of over-training.

Summary

In this chapter, we learned about different AI modeling techniques through two examples—the first with regard to predicting the chances of the borrower going bankrupt and the other with regard to figuring out the funding for the loan. We also learned about reinforcement learning in this chapter. Other artificial intelligence techniques, including deep learning, neural networks, the logistic regression model, decision trees, and Monte Carlo simulation were also covered. We also learned about the business functions of the bank in the context of the examples provided in this chapter.

In the next chapter, we will continue to learn about more AI modeling techniques. We will learn about the linear optimization and linear regression models and use them to solve problems regarding investment banking. We will also learn how AI techniques can become instrumental in mechanizing capital market decisions.

4
Mechanizing Capital Market Decisions

In the previous chapter, we learned about reinforcement learning. We learned how to automate bank decision-making using reinforcement learning. We also learned about AI modeling techniques such as Monte Carlo simulation, the logistic regression model, decision trees, neural networks, and deep learning. We then learned how to build a bankruptcy risk prediction model and used decision-making to fund a loan using reinforcement learning.

In this chapter, we will understand the basic financial and capital market concepts. We will look at how AI can help us in optimizing the best capital structure by running the risk models to generate sales forecasts using macro-economic data. It is useful to plan the internal financial areas of an organization and the external investors' communication. Along with commercial banking activities, which include funding the day-to-day transaction activities of a company, investment banking seeks to pull investors' money behind companies that may want more flexibility in terms of their capital deployment for medium- to long-term activities from these capital-raising markets. We will look at two examples that will help you with financially planning for capital demand.

We will cover the following topics in this chapter:

- Understanding the vision of investment banking
- Basic concepts of the finance domain
- AI modeling techniques
- Finding the optimal capital structure
- Providing a financial performance forecast using macroeconomic scenarios

Let's get started!

Understanding the vision of investment banking

Before we look at the basic concepts of the financial domain, we have to understand the vision of investment banking. The future of investment banking depends on how accurately the future financial performance and behaviors of companies are estimated, as well as how the key factors for the businesses are captured in the model as features. Distributing securities to investors will be automated, as will the syndication desk. The next two chapters will go through the changes that will be made on the client side in regards to their capital decisions, as well as the change on the investment bankers side regarding how to use the model to source investors so that they support the clients' capital needs (clients who raise capital via debt or equity issues are called **issuers**), as well as predicting the M&A needs of clients based on the financial aspects.

Performance of investment banking-based businesses

Once all these predictions are made by machines, automated filing will be implemented via an API that connects firms to the regulators and exchanges. The following diagram shows how issuers, investment bankers, investors/owners, and regulators/exchanges work and coordinate:

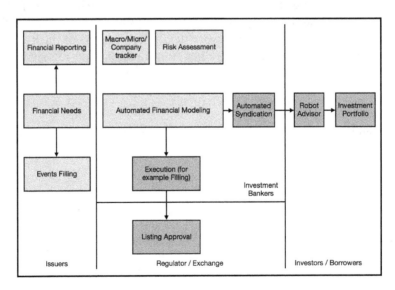

In the preceding diagram, **Issuers** are legal entities associated with registering and selling security. Issuers sell this security in order to finance the operations of the entity. The tasks that issuers have to perform include preparing financial reports and assessing financial needs. The investment bankers facilitate the listing and approval process by performing various operations for issuers.

Basic concepts of the finance domain

In this section, we will look at basic concepts of the finance domain. We will start off by looking at how financial statements are formed. We will also understand the theoretical part of how to optimize capital structure.

Financial statements

Financial statements are used for the health report of a company. A financial report is part of an annual report for the listed company and is the basis of reading the financial health of a company.

Bankers recommend financial products from the results provided in this report, while investors make decisions by referencing this report for investment decisions. With regard to financial statements, there are two major types:

- **Balance sheet**: This is about the overall net worth. It details the total investment (assets), what we owe to the other as debt (for example, credit card and mortgage, liability, and so on), and the net of the investment-less liability, that is, the net worth (equity).
- **Profit and loss account** (**P&L** or income statement): This type shows the dynamics of the financial year. It is like the monthly expenses and income report.

Besides the major types, we also have the following types of financial statements:

- Equity change
- Statement of comprehensive income
- Cash flow statement

These describe the changes in the owner's stakes, the income that wasn't captured in the income statement issue, and cash movement. However, we will not look at these three statements in order to simplify the scope of our examples.

Real-time financial reporting

Every transaction is given as input to the accounting system, while every transaction is classified into an account, which will be classified into one or two of these statements. At the end of the day, each account will be categorized as an account entry.

By analyzing the time series data (in Chapter 2, *Time Series Analysis*), we can clearly see the limitations of the long-range forecast. Therefore, to produce an accurate forecast, our approach shifts to performing frequently updated short-term forecasts. Since we are part of a corporation, it is entirely possible to generate a daily financial statement based on transactional data flowing through the system on a daily basis. For those who have no idea about accounting systems and financial reports, our Excel sheet provides an example of how transaction data gets aggregated as a financial report. The following table shows how the account is classified into the balance sheet and the profit and loss statement:

Item	Asset	Equity	Liability	P&L
Share capital	Y	Y		
Working capital	Y	Y		Y
Capex	Y	Y		Y
Debt capital	Y		Y	
Bank loan	Y		Y	

Share capital is the amount of money (capital means money that is productive) we have contributed to the birth of a company. It's like the resources we receive from parents at birth. It goes to the equity of a company and, naturally, is part of the assets owned by the company. Shareholders are the people who contribute to the capital of the company; thus, they are the owners of the company. A company is expected to pay out dividends (this can be cash or in the form of company shares) to reward investors, mostly on an annual basis. With regard to the money they own in the company, they own everything after repaying what they owe others (as liabilities).

Working capital and capex (capital expenditure) are like our regular recurrent expenses that are required to run our households, such as groceries, bills, and fuel. Think of capex is a major home repair that makes your owned house look better and leads to higher market value, or a new car that you buy to work as an Uber driver (for AI researchers, a GPU computer could be a capex). In this way, anything that impacts P&L will impact equity and assets, which means what we earn as net income will be part of our net worth and our assets. For corporations, capex is spent to acquire properties and equipment.

Liabilities: Debt capital and bank loans are borrowed money and assets. When we borrow these liabilities, they normally come in as cash, but we will immediately pay out this cash for capital expenditure. Bondholders and lenders are people that contribute the debt capital and bank loans to the company. The company is expected to pay the interest (cash) to reward the lenders/bondholders, mostly on a biannual basis. The bond interest is also known as a **coupon**. The amount we borrow is called the **principal**. So, in every borrowing relationship, we have a principal as well as interest.

The objective of the CFO: With different kinds of capital or money, you might be wondering why there is a firm/company in the first place. What is it supposed to do? According to Max Weber (http://sk.sagepub.com/books/writers-on-organizations), a firm is supposed to deliver economic value efficiently by organizing the resources within the firm. So, being a CFO means that we are organizing the financial resources to support the delivery of the firm's major economic activities, which could be generating energy for Duke Energy or organizing goods so that they reach our end customers in supermarkets.

Theories for optimizing the best structure of the firm

The best capital structure is to channel financing to fund the development of the firm while maximizing the investors' investment values with the right risk appetite that best fits the company's business. For example, when the company is in the development stage and the future is unsure, it's better to fund it using the capital that's sticky, that is, equity. When the company becomes stable, it is very common to match it with stable funding, that is, bonds.

What decisions need to be made?

The decision we want to make as a long-term strategic CFO is the right mix of equity and the debt we need to fund the company. On the equity side, we need to consider how many shares we issue to bring in these owners, as well as how many dividends (regular contributions to the investors). On the bond side, we need to consider how many liabilities, what type, what currency, the interest rate, and how long we need for repayment.

Financial theories on capital structure

One great resource for this is *Applied Corporate Finance* by Aswath Damodaran (`https://www.wiley.com/en-us/Applied+Corporate+Finance%2C+4th+Edition-p-9781118808931`). On one hand, a company identifies a project to invest its money into (investment decision), while on the other hand, it arranges financial resources behind it (financing decision). We are not going to identify what project to invest in but how to finance it to make it happen.

According to Bradley, Jarrel, and Kim (`https://econpapers.repec.org/article/blajfinan/v_3a39_3ay_3a1984_3ai_3a3_3ap_3a857-78.htm`), there is an optimal capital mix between equity and liabilities (called **debt**) that will produce the lowest overall financing cost. While there are many reasons for this that have been summarized by Damodaran, let's focus on how to make AI help CFOs in determining an optimal capital structure that is quantifiable and measurable.

As data scientists, we are interested in the cost and benefits of two options, both of which shall help us find the optimal point. Let's take a look:

Why take equity?	Why take debt?
1) No obligation to pay dividends if there's no profit—more flexibility for investment with unclear cash flow visibility such as technology. 2) Increasing equity alone will not raise the cost of equity—approximated as the dividend we pay. However, increasing the debt will increase the probability of company bankruptcy as there is more obligation to repay the interest or principal. 3) More flexibility on certain specifics of financial ratios; for example, some bond borrowers will restrict the company's certain financial ratios to a specific range.	4) Interest paid to lenders is counted as an expense, so there's no need to pay tax, while if paid as a dividend (for the equity holder), it will not be counted as expenses, and therefore, is subject to profit tax. 5) Existing shareholders can retain control of the company without any dilution of ownership.

- Point 1's project certainty on generating a return above the cost of financing can be approximated by the variance of the return.
- Points 2 and 3 can be coded as a formula: for 2, one formula can specify the percentage of debt (called **leverage**) in increasing the risk of bankruptcy (the credit risk model was explained in the previous chapter). For 3, it is just a ratio that can be obtained; that is, the tax rate of the firm.

- Points 4 and 5 can be implemented as a fixed threshold that limits the maximum amount of equity the company can raise. For a family business, a change of equity rarely happens, unless there is a change in the family (for example, the death of the founder).

Total factor productivity to measure project values

This is essentially the question we asked in `Chapter 2`, *Time Series Analysis*, when using time series analysis to automate client procurement and trying to understand how to foresee the demand for each month. For a long-term forecast, we can use the ARIMA model to do the projection. However, there is no clear model when it comes to predicting a project's success within an organization because it requires team members' data, the project's execution, and the type and output of the project, which itself is part of a separate discipline of study in management.

There are three ways we can do this:

- By drawing from insights into the market, we can assume that a project will normally generate the market return on capital—with a floor closed to the risk-free interest rate—if the project has no risk at all. Of course, the return on a higher-risk project shall be higher.
- All in all, if projects are similar to those in the past, the expected value of the project's return shall be the present value of the expected return on the project investment. It has to be equal to the return on the equity of the firm.
- If there has to be a model, drawing from the literature of Marco economics, productivity is measured by the total factor productivity formula:

$$Y = A \times K^{alpha} \times L^{beta}$$

Here, Y is the output, A is the technology's efficiency, K is the capital spent, and L is the labor. The efficiency of capital consumption in terms of financing, purchasing, and sourcing is represented by *alpha*. The labor skills are represented by *beta*. Let's go over these in more detail:

  - A (**technological efficiency**): Technological efficiency could be the ideal economic values delivered by the machine's full handling capacity per dollar spent.
  - L (**labor**): Labor means the ideal economic values delivered by the labor's full handling capacity per dollar spent.

- **K (capital)**: Amount of capital invested in technology and labor.
- *alpha* (**efficiency of capital consumption**): This can be the actual economic value spent on purchaseless profits that are taken by an intermediary and during the process.
- *beta* (**labor skills**): As stated in the book *Human resources and organizational behaviors*, successful project delivery is directly related to the capability of individual members and the roles they play in the team. This can be seen in the growing body of sports results predictions, which can predict the probability of success for each match.

A macroeconomic model is indeed an aggregate behavior of many micro-level behaviors. With regard to the next frontier of macroeconomics, it might make sense for data scientists to draw insights from macroeconomics models that have been applied to individual companies or aggregate micro behaviors to generate macroeconomic behaviors.

If we were to deliver a model that predicts each of the company's project values, we'd often find insights from other disciplines that we could bring in to cross-pollinate the study and quantify it using predictive models. Having the features for this technology, investment amount, and labor might be a good starting point in researching macroeconomics.

Doing this allows us to predict a project's economic values, which in itself can be a machine learning model. We will not cover this here as we wish to focus on high-level financial decisions in this chapter, but the next frontier of finance can generate values.

The cash flow pattern of a project

Besides the productivity/economic value of a project, we also need to find out the precise cash flow payment or receipts of the project. The answer to this is to track all the events of the project from a centralized trusting repository. But wait: for all parties to share information about the same project rather than having a central repository that becomes the central place for hackers, we need a totally decentralized place; this is the rationale of blockchain. The best cash flow pattern prediction comes from getting the data that triggers the cash flow activities: either the project status triggered by signing off progress, confirmation of a sales agreement according to the payment terms, confirming the receipt of goods at a warehouse, and so on.

Practically, in today's world, most of these steps still require human input, so it is easier to ask the relevant human to provide a forward-looking cash flow forecast. Of course, if all these activities become automated and handled by intelligent machines and codified in structured databases, it seems possible to reliably predict future cash flow.

Even if we pass the ball to humans to input data, in finance, we ask humans to provide three scenarios—optimum, realistic, and pessimistic—each with a different probability of occurrence. The expected forecast will be the predicted result of these three scenarios. However, considering the potential issue of an extreme forecast, it seems better to allow humans to make a realistic forecast with an assigned likelihood of such cash flow events to happen within a short time frame.

Again, we are talking about paying large amounts here. For smaller amounts and numerous payments, we have the following approaches:

- Regular cash flow
- Irregular/event-triggered cash flow

Regular cash flow is based on business rules; for example, payroll occurs every Friday. But in order to predict the cash flow of payroll for the next week, we need to get the HR databases, along with the salary for each staff member.

For day-to-day businesses, where regular cash flow is based on expenses paid for procurement and sales made, we can rely on the model we developed in the previous chapter. Once we've projected the demand (sales), we can reliably estimate the procurement required and the corresponding payment being delayed in terms of actual timing—knowing that corporate buyers will delay paying the supplier to earn liquidity. To clarify this, here are a couple of explanations:

- In finance, the ratios of working capital required for sales growth can be calculated by the formula from Churchill N.C. and Mullins, J.W. 2001, *How Fast Can your Company Afford to Grow?* (https://hbr.org/2001/05/how-fast-can-your-company-afford-to-grow).
- Delaying payment may not be optimal for the supply chain since we know that this delayed payment will cause the upstream to further increase their need for short-term financing to fund the production of goods. If the upstream suppliers are smaller in scale, this will actually create a higher overall production cost for the supply chain if the higher-risk/smaller-sized suppliers get financing at a higher rate.

Irregular/event-triggered cash flow: This is usually triggered by other parties or external events. The best way to handle this is to improve data exchange with the customers or suppliers.

Forecasting financial statement items

In this section, we will discuss how we can forecast financial items. Let's take a look:

- **Sales:** If you are a professional trained in finance, the biggest driver—being revenues—has to be forecast based on demand for the goods/services that the company is delivering. In the case of Duke Energy, forecasting the electricity market is basically looking at the market growth of various segments: industrial, commercial, and households. This is the best way to work with marketing.

   In industrial and commercial (B2B) markets, the most reliable forecast is one that looks at the customers; ultimately, the business entity will have to create some goods and services to be consumed by the end customers. For industrial and commercial markets, we can start by looking at the major industrial activities in California and their potential electricity consumption. Then, we move one step forward to observe what they are producing.

   Households depend on the household income, populations, private electric cars, and, most importantly, the weather of the coming years—whether it is El Niño or any other weather forecast, these are important aspects. Even though we can use macroeconomic data (and its forecast, such as the weather forecast) to forecast our sales, it may not always be possible to find predictors for each of the financial items in the financial statements. Here, we can use the known/predictable item to predict the rest, which should make economic and statistical sense.

   In short, the best way to predict sales is to predict the personal sector's sales activities.

- **Cost of goods sold:** This is related to the sales volume. Even though we know that it is not a 1:1 relationship, such as a CFO, we can obtain monthly internal costs and sales figures and build a model to forecast these costs based on sales. Alternatively, we can use demand quantity to forecast procurement quantity. As for Duke Energy, the unit cost also comes largely from commodities markets; given that we have set the target procurement strategy regarding when to buy and the global markets on unit cost are driven by capital markets, we could obtain forward-looking pricing from the markets (that is, CME Henry Hub's 12-month pricing (`https://www.cmegroup.com/trading/energy/natural-gas/natural-gas.html`)).

For companies in the physical goods industry, the cost of goods sold is close to 1:1 to sales if any fixed cost (such as equipment, machinery, and so on) is not allocated to an item. A typical example could be the fashion industry, where the cost of goods sold should align with sales. These sales are proportional to the cost of the goods we purchased.

To illustrate this point, let's run a small analysis on the cost of goods sold versus sales across industries:

SERVICES-NURSING & PERSONAL CARE FACILITIES	-27.38%
SAVINGS INSTITUTION FEDERALLY CHARTERED	0.00%
OIL & GAS FIELD SERVICES NEC	16.88%
CHEMICALS & ALLIED PRODUCTS	34.43%
ELECTRICAL INDUSTRIAL APPARATUS	58.23%
CEMENT HYDRAULIC	79.22%
WHOLESALE-JEWELRY WATCHES PRECIOUS STONES & METALS	99.98%

- **Operating expenses, including selling, general, and administrative expenses (SG&A)**: Depending on the accounting standards and company practice, some companies do not list depreciation and amortization separately, which is not linear to sales activities. Looking at the preceding table, the trend we are seeing is that the higher the fixed asset-intensive industry (called the **capex**), the lower the predictive power of sales to the cost of goods sold. On the other hand, the more human-intensive but less fixed the asset is, the higher the likelihood that the cost of goods sold is moving along due to the higher percentage of variable cost.

AI modeling techniques

In this section, we will look at two important modeling techniques, known as **linear optimization** and the **linear regression model**. In the previous chapter, we learned about deep learning, neural networks, decision trees, and reinforcement learning.

Linear optimization

Used frequently in supply chain businesses, the linear optimization model seeks to achieve the optimization objective (that is, to maximize profit or minimize cost) by changing some variables while considering some constraints. In the case of linear optimization, we also implement the structure similar to that of the capital structure optimization process.

This is not a machine learning model as we do not need to train the machine to learn any patterns.

The linear regression model

This is typically known as the regression model. What it does is find out the causation of some factors of the outcome. The outcome has to be numeric values. In statistics, *some factors* refers to the independent variables as we assume all these factors are independent of other factors, while the outcome is the **dependent variable**. The outcome is dependent on the independent variables.

Finding the optimal capital structure

Now, we can start analyzing how much equity and debt capital we should raise in the capital market to support demand (new projects and businesses or by replacing existing machinery that is worn out or obsolete) and supply (generated from profit). Our projection of optimal capital structure is time-bound; that is, it concerns the optimal mix for a given period, such as the next year. We can certainly expand it to cover the next 5 years. The formula used to forecast business performance is as follows:

*Revenue growth * Fixed Capital Required / Sales*

The optimal capital structure is the capital structure that delivers the lowest possible cost of funding but delivers the required capital to generate values within the firm.

Implementation steps

In this section, we will learn how to implement a machine learning model that can find the optimal capital structure that delivers the lowest possible cost of funding.

Downloading the data and loading it into the model

In our example, we are downloading our data from Quandl, an external financial data provider. This data is quarterly data. Imagine that we are the CFO of a corporation; we can get a real-time daily forecast to update our funding strategy regularly—weekly, monthly, and quarterly. The steps are as follows:

1. Here, we will use *Ticker* to represent the unique identifier of a company. Use the following code to import the required library dependencies:

```
import quandl
import pickle
```

```
import numpy as np
import math
import pandas as pd
from sklearn import linear_model
import matplotlib.pyplot as plt
import seaborn as sns
```

2. Define the API key and a ticker for the company:

```
tkr = 'DUK'
quandl.ApiConfig.api_key = '[API key from Quandl]'
```

3. Download the New York Stock Exchange index values and stock code, and then calculate the return of NYSE versus the stock to come up with beta and risk-free rates for the CAPM pricing model:

```
'''*************************************
## Retrieve data for 2A.
'''
econ = quandl.get("FRED/TEDRATE", authtoken="[API Key from
Quandl]", start_date='2018-05-31', end_date='2018-07-31')
NYSE_index = quandl.get('WFE/INDEXES_NYSECOMPOSITE',
start_date='2013-05-31', end_date='2018-07-31')
```

4. Download the financial data of the company to project and retrieve 2 years' worth of financial data for the target company. This will be fed into the credit model:

```
'''*************************************
## Retrieve Data for the target ticker
'''
record_db = quandl.get_table('SHARADAR/SF1',
calendardate='2017-12-31', ticker=tkr,dimension='MRY')
record_db_t_1 = quandl.get_table('SHARADAR/SF1',
calendardate='2016-12-31', ticker=tkr,dimension='MRY')
```

5. Download the historical financial data of the company in order to estimate the parameters between the driver:

```
'''*************************************
## Download & Load Data for 2C.
'''
tkr = 'DUK'
quandl.ApiConfig.api_key = 'nzBtupqX5H65EG3sFusF'
record_db_t_2017Q1=quandl.get_table('SHARADAR/SF1',
calendardate='2017-3-31', ticker=tkr,dimension='MRQ')
...
df_all = pd.concat(list_all)
```

```
#fix the dataframes

#convert to float

#create new fields

#remove any record with na and 0 values to avoid division errors

#we take a proxy here, should use last period's numbers as
denominator not current period
```

Preparing the parameters and models

In this section, the following parameters will be calculated:

- Levered beta on CAPM in order to calculate the cost of equity.
- Cost of debt by reusing the credit model (the logistic regression model). We're using this because it is simple and requires the least amount of financial ratios.
- Cost of goods sold. The capex is estimated by relating it to sales growth and the cost of goods sold.

With these parameters, it is possible to estimate the major moving parts of the financial model, as follows:

- **Calculate the cost of the equity formula**: Based on the data from 1A, find out the risk-free rate and beta as the intercept and coefficient of the regression formula from the CAPM model: *the Return of Stock = Risk-Free Rate + Beta * Return of Market.*
- **Calculate the cost of the debt formula**: Calculate the cost of debt by calculating the financial ratios. The model we used is based on the 5-year default rate we calculated in the previous chapter. In real life, the bond rating is formulated by the rating agency (such as Moody's or Standard & Poor's), while the bank loan's rating is done internally by the credit risk model of each bank, such as the one we are using.
- Calculate drivers to see how sales can drive other items in the P&L/working capital, directly or indirectly via the cost of goods sold.
- We assume that the cost of goods sold (or the cost of sales) is driven by sales activities, while the operating expense is driven by the cost of sales. We assume that the relationship is linear and can be calculated by the regression model.

- Selling expenses and general and administrative expenses are zero in our example; therefore, we do not have any calculations for them.
- I have also attempted to figure out the relationship between the working capital and receivables, inventory, and payables, but we will not be using it because we will take another approach—the total amount of cash required per sale—to find out the amount of cash/working capital required in the day-to-day operations to support sales.

Projections

Projection involves estimating the revenue growth, followed by looking at the equity and debt capital required that impacts the income statements. Most of the forecasting logics are embedded in `cal_F_WACC`. The optimization result is getting the minimal WACC by trying the range of debt (%) in the capital structure of the company. Unfortunately, we tried this and didn't find it simple to execute through code without implementing a linear optimization algorithm, which will add complexity to the program, even though this is computationally more efficient.

All the stages mentioned in the *Preparing the parameters and models* section are combined. Formulas are built based on the dependency seen in Excel. However, the sequence largely starts with sales, then finding out the capital structure, and then going back to the income statement.

The weighted average costs of the capital are calculated; then, they are compared against the preset conditions, such as the credit risk changed, which cannot be above a certain threshold.

The following are the accounting formulas in forecasting:

- **Sales are projected**: *Sales = Existing Sales * (1 + Sales Growth)*
- **Net income follows the calculation of sales:** *Net Income = Sales - Cost of Good sold - Selling, General Administrative Expenses - Operating Expenses - Net Interest Expense - Taxation Expenses*
    - *Cost of Goods Sold = Sales * Cost to Sales Ratio*
    - *Selling, General Administrative Expenses = Sales * Selling*
    - *General Administrative Expense to Sales Ratio*
    - *Operating Expenses = Sales * Operating Expenses to Sales Ratio*
    - *Net Interest Expense = Debt * Interest Expense%*

- **The equity and debt in total we need equates to the capital required**: *Equity + Debt >= Existing PPE + New PPE Needed + Working Capital Required + Inventory + Goodwill*
  - *Equity = Existing Equity + New Equity Capital Generated*
  - *Debt = Existing Debt + New Net Debt Capital Generated*
  - *New Capital Required = New Equity Capital Required + New Debt Capital Required*
  - *New Net Equity Capital Generated = New Equity Capital Raised - Divided Payment + New Equity from Earnings*
  - *New Equity Capital Generated from Earnings = Net Income*
  - *New Net Debt Capital Generated = New Debt Capital Raised - Debt Repayment*
  - *Debt Repayment = Previous Debt Repayment*
  - *Total Property Plant and Equipment (PPE) Needed = Existing PPE (net of depreciation) - Depreciation for the Next Period + New PPE Needed*
  - *Sales / Total PPE Needed = Sales to PPE Ratio*
  - *Working Capital Required = Working Capital Required per Sales * Sales*
  - *Working Capital Required per Sales = Cost of Sales/Sales * Total Cash Cycle in Days/ Operating Cash Cycle in Days + Operation Expenses / Sales * 1/2*

The code for this is as follows:

```
'''************************************
3. Projection
'''
print('optimization...')
#simulations
record_db_f = record_db

#Projection
...

def cal_F_WACC(record_db_f, logreg, logreg_sc,
new_debt_pct,price_offering,levered_beta,sales_growth,coefs,r_free):
...
for new_debt_pct in debt_pct_range:
 for price_offering in price_offering_range:
 ...
 F_WACC, F_default_risk,conditions =
cal_F_WACC(record_db_f,logreg,logreg_sc, new_debt_pct,
price_offering,levered_beta,sales_growth,coefs,r_free)
 '''************************************
 4. Calculate WACC
 '''
```

```
#update WACC
obj = F_WACC < optimal_WACC and
F_default_risk/default_risk_existing-1<=0.75
 ...
```

Calculating the weighted average cost of capital

The objective of this step is to ensure the following happens:

- The ideal capital structure is rewarded by the lowest cost of capital with a mix of debt and equity.
- The cost of equity is defined by the capital asset pricing model.
- The cost of debt is defined by the cost of credit risk, plus the cost of the risk-free rate. The cost of credit risk is calculated by the credit model we built in the previous chapter.
- Minimize the following:
    - **Weighted Average Cost of Capital (WACC)**
    - Cost of debt
    - Cost of credit risk
    - Cost of equity
    - Unlevered beta
    - Levered beta

Constraints used in optimization

Let's take a look at the demand and supply of capital, which has to be tied up:

- **Restrictions on capital mix**: The existing bondholder does not want the rating to be altered; therefore, they are limited to changing the default risk by less than 75%.
- **Constraints calculated but not checked for optimization**:
    - These restrictions are not implemented because there will be circular references to profit and loss items that shall be fixed.
    - Normally, these are the constraints imposed by the existing shareholders.
    - The existing shareholders don't want the earnings per share to be dropped as there are more shares.
    - The existing shareholders don't want to chip in the extra equity to the same company by drastically increasing the equity amount.

The following code snippet demonstrates how equity offering constraints are calculated:

```
#equity offering constraints --- not bounding
price_offering = record_db_f['price'][0]
unit_offering = int(F_new_equity / price_offering)
F_eps = F_earnings / (unit_offering+record_db_f['shareswa'][0])
equity_growth = F_equity / record_db_f['equity'][0]-1
eps_growth = abs(F_eps/
(record_db_f['netinc'][0]/record_db_f['shareswa'][0])-1)
c_eq_1 = equity_growth <= 0.1
c_eq_2 = eps_growth <= 0.3
```

Congratulations! We have found the optimal capital structure for the company using optimization.

Providing a financial performance forecast using macroeconomic scenarios

One of the key jobs of a CFO is to provide a forecast for financial performance. So, how is AI going to change this job? We will build on what we know about finance in terms of helping with financial projections for accounting rules between items and add the predictive capability of our age to improve it.

As the CFO of the listed firm, one of our key aspects is to provide management and analyst guidance for forward-looking financials. Hypothetical data is handcrafted by the author. This seeks to emulate what the accounting system looks like.

In this section, we will look at how to forecast the financial performance of the firm.

Implementation steps

In this section, we will learn how to derive financial performance forecasts using macroeconomic scenarios. The steps are as follows:

1. Initialize the tickers in each industry by loading them from CSV files and importing the required library dependencies:

```
from pyquery import PyQuery
import pandas as pd
import quandl
import matplotlib.pyplot as plt
from sklearn import linear_model
```

```
from sklearn.metrics import r2_score

...
```

2. Download the historical financial data from Quandl:

```
cal_LIND = quandl.get("FRED/CASLIND",
authtoken="nzBtupqX5H65EG3sFusF")
cal_ele =
quandl.get(["EIA/ELEC_SALES_CA_RES_M","EIA/ELEC_SALES_CA_IND_M"],
authtoken="nzBtupqX5H65EG3sFusF")
```

3. Calculate the various parameters required to derive the performance:

```
#update the index date to begin of month (in fact all index should
be referring to end of month)
cal_ele['mth_begin'] = cal_ele.index
#change the column to begin of month
...

reg_retail = linear_model.LinearRegression()
reg_retail.fit(df_marco[[' MeanAvgTemperature']], \
                df_marco['EIA/ELEC_SALES_CA_RES_M - Value'])
reg_retail.coef_
reg_retail_pred = \
            reg_retail.predict(df_marco[['MeanAvgTemperature']])
error_retail = r2_score(df_marco['EIA/ELEC_SALES_CA_RES_M - \
                                    Value'], reg_retail_pred)

reg_ind = linear_model.LinearRegression()
reg_ind.fit(df_marco[[' MeanAvgTemperature']], \
                df_marco['EIA/ELEC_SALES_CA_IND_M - Value'])
reg_ind.coef_
reg_ind_pred = reg_ind.predict(df_marco[['MeanAvgTemperature']])
error_ind = r2_score(df_marco['EIA/ELEC_SALES_CA_IND_M - \
                                    Value'], reg_ind_pred)
...
```

Congratulations! You have generated the sales forecast using macro factors that have been reliably forecast by meteorological experts.

Summary

In this chapter, we looked at financial banking and a few basic concepts of the finance domain. We learned about two important machine learning modeling techniques known as optimization and the linear regression model. We also looked at two examples that help automate capital market decisions—*Finding optimal capital structure* and *Providing a financial performance forecast using macroeconomic scenarios*. We also looked at the future and the implications of investment banking and financial reporting.

Then, we explored the internals of financial projection and financial modeling, which we were able to do due to financial positions being rapidly updated with real-time financial IT systems. By leveraging the richness of financial positions on a daily basis, we have lots of data points to perform a reliable projection of the complete financial positions of a firm. Being the strategic thinkers of the firm, we also looked at how to rely on external data (such as weather data from popular forecasting services from the government) to augment the lack of internal financial data as a CFO. We leveraged an external data provider called Quandl to blend all the financial data from peers in the same industry. In reality, this technique should be replaced by an internal position snapshot, but essentially, the key point is to blend AI with financial modeling.

As you can see, the future of financial reporting may have to dive deeper than just reporting financial statements. CFOs may be required to disclose the project's status and plan for greater transparency, as well as the benefits of the investors, without jeopardizing commercial secrecy. This form of disclosure is also present in annual reports but isn't in a quantitative format yet. The CFOs of the future will have to buckle up for this new wave of reporting philosophy as what happens inside the organization is what is driving the return of capital.

In the next chapter, we will continue learning about new machine learning techniques that will help us solve complex financial problems. We will also understand a core business concept known as **Merger and Acquisition (M&A)**. We will understand the basic concepts of data technologies such as SQL and look at a machine learning modeling technique known as **clustering models**.

5
Predicting the Future of Investment Bankers

In the previous chapter, we understood the basic financial and capital market concepts. We looked at how AI can help us in optimizing the best capital structure by running risk models and generating sales forecasts using macro-economic data. We also looked at how useful AI is while planning the financial internals of an organization and external investors' communication. We then looked at two examples – the first regarding how to optimize the funding mix of debt and equity and the second regarding performing a financial forecast that could help us with financially planning capital demand.

The goal of this chapter is to introduce additional techniques that can be used for financial planning. You will learn how to perform auto syndication for new issues so that the capital can be obtained from the interested investors. Then, you will learn how to identify acquirers and targets, a process that requires a science background so that you can pick the ones that need the banking services the most.

In this chapter, we will cover the following topics:

- Basics of investment banking
- Understanding data technologies
- Clustering models
- Auto syndication for new issues
- Identifying acquirers and targets

Let's get started!

Basics of investment banking

Investment banking will be the focus of this chapter. Therefore, you will need to understand a few basic concepts surrounding investment banking. We will begin by understanding the challenges of an **Initial Public Offer**, commonly known as an **IPO**. When a company decides to go to the stock market in order to acquire money from the public, they release an IPO for the public and institutions to subscribe to. We will also understand the concepts of M&A, as well as how to classify investors and apply AI to mergers and acquisitions.

The job of investment bankers in IPOs

The following are some of the core problems that investment bankers deal with:

- **Pricing:** What is the right price for the new issuance (of equity)?
- **Syndication:** Who should we distribute the shares to and at what price?
- **Listing:** How can we register these shares with the markets (such as stock exchanges) so that they pass all the requirements as investment security in the market?

Let's answer each of these questions, one by one.

To answer the first question, in the previous chapter, we briefly illustrated how to correctly model the capital structure of the company, including its financial position. The core of this remains how to estimate the drivers when given some macro indicators that matter to the company concerned.

To answer the second question, it makes a difference if we have visibility of the investment preference of the market. When the investment decision on investors is automated by the robot adviser, we should find it easy to test the demand of the investors represented by the robot. The robot needs parameters on the investment, while lots of these projections are made by an investment bank's engine; that is, its past accuracy shall also be considered when accessing information (also known as **the prospectus**) about potential issues. We will address this question in the first example we will complete in this chapter.

The third question focuses a lot on reporting and filing information regarding the legitimacy of the company's ownership and legal status, as well as its risk factors. When this issue is executed by a robot, there will be different requirements from the regulator/stock exchange:

- There should be a robot from the regulator/stock exchange side to validate the claims of the filing company. Here, a robot indicates an intelligent software program that can perform specific tasks meant for it. However, it may even be possible for the listing company's CFO to upload their sales forecast as per what we discussed in `Chapter 4`, *Mechanizing Capital Market Decisions*. The material factor that impacts the sales of an electricity company is the weather, given that it is highly predictive of its sales.
- Besides factors related to its sales, risk factors include other macroeconomics variables that impact the major financial items of financial statements. Factors sensitive to the firm's strategies will be covered in the second example of `Chapter 7`, *Sensing Market Sentiment for Algorithm Marketing at the Sell-Side*. We will do this here since the investor-side also influences the important topics that need to be focused on.

Stock classification – style

There are two schools of thought when it comes to classifying stocks: one based on qualitative features and another based on quantitative features. We will be focusing on the qualitative approach, which is called **style**. An example of such a scheme is *Morningstar Style Box* (`http://news.morningstar.com/pdfs/FactSheet_StyleBox_Final.pdf`).

Here, we can look at the sector/industry, the size of the stocks, the riskiness of the stock, the potential of the stock, and so on. There are many ways to create features and classify stocks. We will use sector and size as the features for qualitative classification in this chapter.

The quantitative approach (for example, **arbitrage pricing theory** (**APT**)) groups stocks that contain similar factors together analytically.

Investor classification

Like stock classification, there are both quantitative and qualitative approaches. Qualitative could be based on the type of money (pension, sovereign wealth, insurance, and so on), strategies (long-short, global macro, and so on), underlying holdings (futures, commodities, equities, bonds, and private equities), riskiness, and so on. Quantitative could be based on proximate factors that these investors are based on. In the first example of this chapter, we will use investment riskiness and return as the features for qualitative classification.

Mergers and acquisitions

Investment banking covers not just listing securities but also advisory services such as **mergers and acquisitions (M&A)**, financial opinions such as company valuation, and other event-driven financing operators such as management buyout. In short, all these activities deal with buying and selling companies and/or company assets and pricing them correctly. The easiest way to understand this is by thinking about property brokers, appraisers, and mortgage bankers in terms of buying a house. M&A is like two people getting married – sometimes, one will be more dominant, while other times, it is a marriage of two equal entities. The rationale behind this is that a firm exists because it is more efficient to operate, as theorized by Ronald Coase in 1937. As technologies, regulations, and consumer preferences change, the economic boundary of a firm changes too, which makes the case for M&A.

We are largely talking about the following types of transactions:

- Acquisition (acquiring another firm)
- Merger (two or more firms combine)
- Divestiture (sell itself)
- Spin-off (selling part of the firm), and so on

Another dimension of classifying M&A is done through the pre-deal relationship between the acquirers and the target: if they are both in the same industry, this is called **horizontal integration**; if they are in a supplier-customer relationship, this is called **vertical integration**; when neither of them are linked, this is called **diversification**.

As an investment banker, these are the key areas you need to look into:

- **Predeal matter**: Ensure the commitment/willingness of the acquirer and the target to embark on a journey together to explore a deal.
- **Approvals**: Approval by regulators or existing shareholders.
- **Postdeal matter**: Deliver 1 + 1 > 2. This is not because of bad math; this is because certain processes are more integrated to deliver better results. So, when two entities (companies) are added together, the cost will be lower or the revenue will be higher.

According to the guide for dummies (`https://www.dummies.com/business/corporate-finance/mergers-and-acquisitions/steps-of-the-ma-process/`), an M&A deal can be summarized with the following steps:

1. Contact the targets
2. Exchange documents and pricing
3. Conduct due diligence
4. Close the deal
5. Perform post-deal integration

Next, we'll look at the application of AI in M&A.

Application of AI in M&A

With regard to the application of AI for bankers, AI is used to identify the right target and help quantify the pricing for post-deal synergies. Both of these steps (the first and the last step) are highly unreliable under the existing setting, where there is not much science involved. Firstly, bankers' time is very expensive, while the mortality rate of any prospection deal is very high (for example, 90%). Clients (buyer/seller) will have the incentive of maximizing the banker's service hours, even though no deal may be closed. Given the banker's limited time and clients' conflicting goal of maximizing the banker's time, regardless of their actual intention to close any deal, the best approach is to find the actual economics derived from the M&A deal. If it works fundamentally, there shall be a higher urgency to announce and engage the investment bankers on deal execution/announcement.

The modeling approach actually exists today in credit risk modeling, which we mentioned in the previous chapters. Given the financials, we predict a binary outcome regarding whether an event occurs or not. In the case of the credit risk model, there is bankruptcy occurrence within X years; whereas, for mergers, it could be an acquisition or divestment announcement within X years given the financials. I personally do not see any difference between these modeling approaches if the probability of bankruptcy can be estimated as such.

Secondly, when it comes to quantifying post-deal synergies, there is either cost-efficiency, revenue growth, or higher productivity with a better mix of knowledge transfer by the staff:

- When it comes to cost-efficiency, we can easily run the sales analysis for the cost relationship in the industry to quantitatively validate whether it is the actual behavior of the industry or just some wishful thinking that the suppliers will accept lower payment from the combined company.
- With regard to revenue synergies, this is a massive data exchange exercise and can only be done with proper machine learning models. For example, if the synergy is about better market access (for example, competitor A, a buyer, buying competitor B in the same industry), the targeting model of competitor A shall be run on competitor B's customer database to derive how much revenue will likely be generated. This happens with joint database marketing programs; for example, insurance distributed via banks (**Bancassurance**). Here, the insurers provide the model to run on the bank's customer database.
- For know-how related to human resources synergies, I see an equal possibility of applying HR analytics to measure and quantify knowledge, skill level and cultural fitness, and team performance. The hard and soft side of the staff shall be measured, projected, and simulated in the pre-due synergy analysis.

To do this, I do not believe that any existing M&A banker would be willing to change much because the time spent on doing this would be rather long given that, right now, the extent of digitalization for customers and staff is not yet mainstream. This means that features and models can't do this. But I do believe that we should work on this future model of M&A, especially now that we are building the future of M&A and training the next generation.

Compared to a financial investment, M&A has a huge uncertainty in terms of it operational integration, which is exactly where AI should deliver value. Numerous studies have been conducted on the determinant factors of a successful M&A deal that deliver the promised synergies; these findings or features from academic researches need to be collected and run through in order to generate a quantifiable success likelihood and will be priced while calculating the offering price.

Filing obligations of listing companies

To ensure there are fair markets for the investors of publicly listed securities, the exchange requires that we announce the occurrence of events such as the release of financial results, major company activities that affect the valuation of security, and so on. For example, you can refer to the *New York Stock Exchange's IPO guide* (`https://www.nyse.com/publicdocs/nyse/listing/nyse_ipo_guide.pdf`).

Understanding data technologies

We are going to manage a large amount of data through the examples in this chapter. Due to this, it is critical to understand the underlying data technologies that we will use. These data technologies are related to storing varying types of data and information. There are two challenges related to information storage – first is the physical medium that we use to store the information, while the second is the format in which the information is stored.

Hadoop is one such solution that allows stored files to be physically distributed. This helps us to deal with various issues such as storing a large amount of data in one place, backup, recovery, and so on. In our case, we store the data on one computer as the size does not justify using this technology, but the following NoSQL databases could support this storage option. In Python, there is another file format called **HDF5**, which also supports distributed filesystems.

While NoSQL databases can be used, the reason why I am not using them in this chapter can be explained with the help of the following table, which compares SQLite, Cassandra, and MongoDB side by side:

	Pros	Cons	Conclusions
SQLite	Structured data format, compatible with DataFrames	Cannot save unstructured data.	We need this for simplicity.
Cassandra	Can run at distributed computing and can put in structured data (with fields as items)	When dealing with structured data, the syntax is not straightforward to insert.	We can't use these for our case as we aim to cluster similar investors and predict who will buy our new issues in IPO.
MongoDB	Can handle huge data sizes and parallel processing of different records at scale	Not suitable for fully structured data such as trading records; still need to convert it into a DataFrame before running any machine learning algorithm.	

Through this analysis, we see that it may not be necessary to have a NoSQL database for the sake of being cutting-edge. In the case of capital markets, where data is quite structured, it could be more efficient to use a SQL database that fits this purpose.

Clustering models

Before we start looking at the programming content, let's take a look at clustering models, since we will be using one in our first example.

Clustering seeks to group similar data points together. As a simple example, when there are three data points, each with one column, [1],[2],[6], respectively, we pick one point as the centroid that represents the nearby points; for example, with two centroids, [1.5] and [5], each represents a cluster: one with [1],[2] and another cluster with [6], respectively. These sample clusters can be seen in the following diagram:

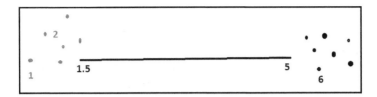

When there are two columns for each data point, the distance between the actual data point and the centroid needs to consider the two columns as one data point. We adopt a measurement called **Euclidean distance** for this.

One of the key challenges of adopting clustering in banking is that it leads to clusters that are too large, which reduces the true positive rate if all the clusters are targeted. As per my experience, I would use it for preliminary data analysis to understand the major dynamics of the target populations, not necessarily to draw actionable insights that make economic sense in a wholesale banking setting. In our example, we will create lots of clusters with the very stringent requirement that the distance of each data point from the centroid averages a 5% deviation.

Another key question regarding the clustering algorithm is determining how many features we feed it. We could commit bias clustering by overweighing certain types of financial ratios (for example, using two different kinds of profitability ratios, such as return on equity and return on asset) for clustering. The solution to this is to run principle component analysis, which removes similar features by merging them into the same feature.

For a non-finance/banking example, you can refer to *Building Recommendation Engines* by Suresh Kumar Gorakala (`https://www. packtpub.com/big-data-and-business-intelligence/building-practical-recommendation-engines-part-1-video`).

Auto syndication for new issues

If there are issues, there are investors behind them. Traditional investment banks will hire a group of professionals called the **syndication desk** to handle the allocation of security issues to investors who can buy these shares and bonds.

If we consider the role of the syndication desk of the investment bank, our work will be to identify the cornerstone investors of the upcoming new issues with Duke Energy, as the CFO has the funding needs in equities. To do so, we will use the institutional holding data of US stocks from SEC filing via Quandl/Sharadar, which will help us find out the investment preferences of investors who share similar interests and match those with the investors who also hold similar stocks, such as Duke Energy.

With regard to who to sell to, we will take the largest investors of US stocks as our universe of investors. The syndicated desk's job is to sell the major position of any equity issues to these investors. Using the unsupervised learning method, we recommend the relevant stocks to the right investors as an initial public offering. This can be done using securities similarities (called **holding similarities**) and investment styles (called **investor similarities**).

Solving the problem

The following diagram shows the steps involved in solving the problem at hand:

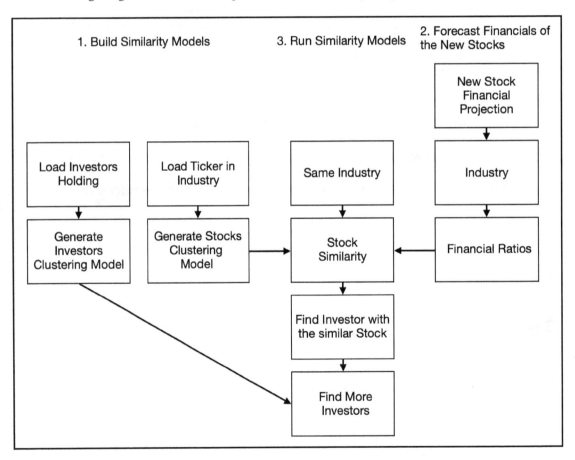

We will cover each step in detail in the following sections.

Building similarity models

Here, we will build two similarity models – one on stock similarity and another on finding similar investors. Both models are clustering models, and they belong to the last type of machine learning approach – unsupervised learning. We have picked 21 financial ratios to build the clustering model at the stock level, while for the investor model, we have a maximum of 60 features (*six capitalization sizes * five investment decisions * two types of indicators*):

- Six capitalization scales: Nano, Micro, Small, Medium, Large, and Mega
- Five investment decisions: Two for Buy (New, or Partial), one for Hold, and two for Sell (All or Partial)
- Seven indicators: Quarterly return (total return, realized, unrealized), new money changing rate's mean and standard deviation, and current value

Import all the relevant libraries and then load the ticker's universe by reading the CSV files together with the scale fields that describe the stocks. To reduce the processing time, load the investor lists instead of all the investors. For each investor, calculate the direction per market segment stock (that is, we use scale as the only market segment, but in reality, we should use country × industry × scale).

Building the investor clustering model

To build an investor clustering model, loop through the investors and calculate the movement and the profit (realized and unrealized profit), as follows:

1. Import the required libraries and data:

```
'''***********************
Load Data
'''
#import relevant libraries
import quandl
from datetime import date,timedelta
import pandas as pd
import os

#load tickers universe and description field (scale)
...

#loop through investors
...

for investor in investorNameList:
```

```
...
#calculate the change in position by ticker on
 Quarter-to-quarter basis
...

#qualify investor's activities
print('classify investor decision')
...
#output the ticker's activities of the investor
```

2. Prepare the investor profiles:

```
## Prepare investor Profile'''
#load relevant libraries
import os
import pandas as pd
import numpy as np
from time import time
from sklearn import metrics
from sklearn.cluster import KMeans
from sklearn.preprocessing import StandardScaler
import pickle


...

#Summarize quarterly performance of investors per quarter
...
for file in file_list:
    ...
    for index, row in tmp_pd.iterrows():
        ...

    #calculate return (realized, unrealized and new money)
    ...
```

3. Prepare the cluster investors, as well as the output clusters and results:

```
## Cluster investors
#cleansed and transform data for clustering
...

sc_X = StandardScaler()
X = sc_X.fit_transform(investor_pd)

#define the k means function
def bench_k_means(estimator, name, data):
    ...
```

```
#try out different K means parameters and find out the best
parameters
...

for num_cluster in range(5, 500):
    KMeans_model = KMeans(init='k-means++', \
                          n_clusters=num_cluster, n_init=10)
    ...

## Output the results
#Output clusters
```

Here, we run clustering analysis on the features that list the realized and unrealized return by market. Then, we set a threshold of 0.05, which means that the clusters that we build have to have 5% variation across the feature variables. Finally, we output the clustering results; that is, the clustering results, the clustering model, and the scaler.

Building the stock-clustering model

To build the stock-clustering model, we will load the data, prepare the stock's profile, cluster the stock, and output the clusters and results:

1. Load the industry, tickers, and functions and import the libraries and the KPI key for Quandl:

```
'''**************************************
i. load industry, tickers and functions
'''
#import libraries
import quandl
import pandas as pd
import numpy as np
import os
from time import time
from sklearn import metrics
from sklearn.cluster import KMeans
from sklearn.preprocessing import StandardScaler
import pickle

#KPI keys
...

...
```

2. Use `sklearn` to run the training models. Use `pickle` to load up the results and models. Then, download the fundamental data of the ticker for the latest annual financials:

```
#define important functions
#download fundamental data of the ticker
def download_tkr(tkr):
    ...
```

3. Define the required *k* means clustering functions. Filter the industry by using tickers exceeding a cutoff. Here, we will use 100 tickers as the cutoff. When assessing the industry, we list the clusters in the industry. Then, download the financial data from the industry that passes this threshold. For each of the tickers in the industry cluster, clean the data type:

```
#kmean clustering function
def bench_k_means(estimator, name, data):
    ...


''' **********************************
#2a. load data
'''
#parameters
...


''' **********************************
#i. filter the industry in scope
'''

...


#collect tkr in each industry
for index, row in df_tkr.iterrows():
    ...
```

4. Then, calculate the clustering model of the industry. The maximum number of clusters should be half of the total number of tickers in the industry. The clustering model will stop if it reaches the maximum silhouette score of 5%, which is the target, or when it reaches $N/2$ clusters (N = number of tickers in the industry):

```
''' **********************************
#ii. create a dataframe for each industry to do clustering
'''

...
#loop through the industry
```

```
for ind, list_tkr in dict_ind_tkr.items():
    ...
    #Go through the ticker list to Download data from source
    #loop through tickers from that industry
    for tkr in list_tkr:
        ...
    '''*************************************
    2b. prepare features for clustering for the industry
    '''
    #convert to float and calc the difference across rows
    ...
    '''*************************************
    2C. Perform K means clustering for the industry
    '''
    #clustering
    sc_X = StandardScaler()
    X = sc_X.fit_transform(df_fs_filter)


    ...
    for num_cluster in range(5, max_clsuter):
        KMeans_model = KMeans(init='k-means++', \
                            n_clusters=num_cluster, n_init=10)
        ...
```

5. Output the scalar, clustering model, and the result of clustering:

```
'''*************************************
2D. Output the clustering model and scaler for the industry
'''
#Output clusters
...
```

By adopting the methodology we developed in the previous chapter on financial projection, we can derive the financial statements and hence the financial ratios used for classifying the stock later.

In the example we looked at in the previous chapter, we projected the capital structure after issuing debt and equity. But to begin with, we did not assume any movement in stock price, for example, P/E ratios, except movement in profitability, scale, and so on.

To forecast the financials of the new stock, perform the following steps:

1. Import all the relevant libraries and use `pickle` to load the results and models:

```
#import relevant libraries
import os
import pickle
import math
import numpy as np
import pandas as pd
import quandl
```

   ...

2. Leverage the program we built in the previous chapter and run the financial projection defined in the preceding section. Then, calculate the metrics of the projected financials for the company to be listed:

```
#perform financial projection
#reuse the function developed for WACC optimization
def cal_F_financials(record_db_f, logreg, logreg_sc, new_debt_pct,
price_offering, levered_beta, sales_growth, coefs, r_free):
    ...


'''******************************
Step 2: Simulate financial of the new stock
'''

...

#load credit model built previously
...

#reuse the parameters developed from WACC example
...

#assume that we are raising equity for the same client
...

#run simulation / projection of financial data
...
```

As we can see, the stock clusters look like the new stock we are working on. The clustering model will tell us which other stocks in the same cluster this new stock is associated with.

There is a shortcut we can use when building the model on stocks, which is also a practical consideration. For stocks in an industry that has too few stocks (less than 100, for example), there is no need to build a clustering model to help us find the subgroups within the industry. Instead, we should go and check every single stock if there aren't many of them.

Given the complete member list of the stock clusters, we can go to the existing stockholders of these stocks to find out the current owners (investor list A). If we still need more names to approach, then we can run another investor-level clustering model to find out who else (investor list B) might be interested in this stock that shares similar traits as investor list A.

Follow these steps to perform clustering:

1. Find the stocks that have similar financials to the one we are looking to list/syndicate and which share the same industry.
2. Based on the stocks we found, we find out who the existing holders of the stocks are.
3. We find the list of investors who hold the stocks we checked; that is, the selected investors.
4. We find the clustering IDs of all the investors.
5. Given the selected investors, find out clusters and the other investors that share the same cluster ID. Those are the target investors we will sell the new issue to.

The following is the pseudocode we can use to perform clustering:

```
#Step 2 and 3. Perform clustering to find out the similar investors whose
sharing the similar stocks


'''****************************
Step 3: Run the similarity models to find out holders of the similar stocks
'''
#check if we need any model - if industry has too few stocks, no model
needed to find out the similar stocks
...

#retrieve the list of tickers that are similar
...


#find list of investors looking at the similar size and more
#check which investors have it...
...


#loop through investors holding name by name to find out investor that is
holding the similar stocks
for filename in investorNameList:
```

```
    . . .

#Load the investor clustering model
. . .
#extract the investors' cluster id
. . .

#find out who else share the same cluster id
. . .

#print out the investor list
. . .
```

The preceding code shows how to list the clustered investors with similar portfolio stocks. Here, we have built a clustered model for investors and used it. In the next section, we will build an understanding of acquirers and targets.

Identifying acquirers and targets

There has been a long history of corporate finance research in the field of acquirers and targets, and our challenge is to apply this rich body of research to the real world. Hedge funds have been applying these research findings as merger arbitrage, and M&A bankers have always had their eyes on scoring and assessing the market on a regular basis (for example, reading the morning news).

In this chapter, we will assume that you are an M&A banker looking for organization opportunities. To optimize our time allocation, we can allocate our time better by focusing on clients that can close the deal. Therefore, we will use a model to predict the probability of us being the acquirers or targets in M&A.

The current new generation of investment bankers should use automated financial modeling tools. Over time, data can be captured, and then prediction capability can be added to assist bankers in financial modeling. The current world, which uses Excel, definitely needs to do more NLP research into how to train a machine to parse/understand an Excel-based financial model, which is understood by humans but barely understood by the machine at all!

Secondly, an M&A prediction model should be part of the investment committee/mandate acceptance committee, where the likelihood of announcing the deal shall be presented – just like how credit ratings are presented in credit committees today.

So, let's see how we can apply a similar approach to credit rating in M&A prediction to spot a deal.

Follow these steps to solve this problem. We will start by loading the necessary Python libraries:

1. Import all the required libraries and define the key variables:

```
'''**************************************
#1. Import libraries and define key variables
'''
import pandas as pd
import numpy as np
import quandl
import matplotlib.pyplot as plt
from sklearn.metrics import classification_report,roc_curve,
auc,confusion_matrix,f1_score
from sklearn.model_selection import train_test_split
from sklearn import tree
from sklearn.neural_network import MLPClassifier
from sklearn.preprocessing import StandardScaler
import pickle
import graphviz

#KPI keys
quandl.ApiConfig.api_key = '[API Key for Quandl]'
```

2. Download the financials of a given ticker (leverage them from the previous example) and define the function you will use to train the tree and the neural network, including grid search (all of these can be leveraged from `Chapter 3`, *Using Features and Reinforcement Learning to Automate Bank Financing*):

```
'''**************************************
#2. Definition of functions
'''
#2a.Download tickers
def download_tkr(tkr):
...
#2b.Train tree
def train_tree(X,Y,ind):
...
##2C Neural Network
#2Ci. Grid search that simulate the performance of different neural
network design
def grid_search(X_train,X_test,
Y_train,Y_test,num_training_sample):
...
#2Cii. Train Neural Network
def train_NN(X,Y,ind):
...
```

3. Filter the industries that have a sizable number of tickers and run through the industry and its respective tickers to build the decision tree and the neural network:

```
def filterIndustriesByTickets(ind):
```

4. Output the results by the ROC curve per industry:

```
def displayCurveChart(type, ind):
```

5. Load the list of companies from the file alongside their sectors, just like we did auto syndication. Select the sectors that have at least 30 companies to ensure size. Load the tickers of the same sector into one entry on a dictionary, taking the sector as the key and tickers as values:

```
'''*************************************
3. Execute the program
#3a. filter the industry in scope
'''
groupby_fld = 'sicsector'
min_size = 30
df_tkr = pd.read_csv('industry_tickers_list.csv')
...
#collect ticker in each industry
for index, row in df_tkr.iterrows():
    ind = row[groupby_fld]
    tkr = row['ticker']
    if ind in list_scope:
        if ind in dict_ind_tkr:
            dict_ind_tkr[ind].append(tkr)
        else:
            dict_ind_tkr[ind] = [tkr
```

6. Loop through the selected sectors one by one and load the companies' historical financials. For each company, we will load 10 year's worth of annual financial records:

```
#loop through the dictionary - one industry at a time
for ind, list_tkr in dict_ind_tkr.items():
    df_X = pd.DataFrame({})
    df_Y = pd.DataFrame({})
    print(ind)
    #Go through the ticker list to Download data from source
    #loop through tickers from that industry
    for tkr in list_tkr:
        print(tkr)
        try:
```

```
df_tmp,X_tmp,Y_tmp = download_tkr(tkr)
...
```

Here, we loaded the events of the company. After loading the events, we filtered only those related to M&A and made them a binary column to denote whether the company has completed any M&A within 1 calendar year, where 1 equals yes. Then, we joined both company financials and events together—we joined both *t-1* years financials with the binary event indicator at year *t*. We converted the null event into *0*. Most of this logic is implemented to prepare the financials and events, which is done via `download_tkr(tkr)`.

7. Split the data from the industry in order to train the models:

```
#neural network
nn_clf,f1_score_temp = train_NN(df_X,df_Y,ind)
f1_list.append(f1_score_temp)
nn_clf.get_params()
#decision tree
try:
    tree_clf,f1_score_temp = train_tree(df_X,df_Y,ind)
except Exception:
    continue
f1_list.append(f1_score_temp)
tree_clf.get_params()
```

Here, we leveraged what we built in `Chapter 2`, *Time Series Analysis*. However, for the sake of illustration, we only used a decision tree and neural network code.

This brings us to the end of this chapter.

Summary

In this chapter, you understood the basics of investment banking. Now, you should be able to understand the concepts of IPO and M&A. Based on the data technologies you learned about in this chapter, you should be able to model the domain requirements. With the use of the clustering model technique, you can now create high-performance artificial intelligence systems.

After this, we completed an exercise where we solved the problem of auto syndication for new issues. We also looked at an example regarding how to identify acquirers and targets.

In the next chapter, we will focus on portfolio management, asset management, and a few artificial techniques that are suitable in the domain of portfolio management.

6
Automated Portfolio Management Using Treynor-Black Model and ResNet

In the previous chapter, we covered the basic concepts of investment banking. We also learned about the concepts of **Mergers and Acquisitions (M&A)** and **Initial Public Offering (IPO)**. We examined the clustering model, which is a modeling technique of AI. We looked at detailed steps and examples to solve the problem with auto syndication. We implemented an example that identified acquirers and targets. So, the previous two chapters were intended for the issuers on the securities side of investment banking.

In this chapter, we will look at the dynamics of investors. Investors drive investment behavior strategically. The issuance of equity or debt can be done in either of two ways—via the primary market or the secondary market. The role of the primary market is to issue new securities on behalf of companies, the government, or other groups in order to receive financing by debt or equity-oriented securities. The role of the secondary market is to facilitate interested parties with the buying or selling of previously issued securities. The role of portfolio managers is to make smarter decisions based on the price movement of the securities to increase the amount of profit for their customers. The portfolio manager tries to understand the needs of investors and places money behind those investments that generate the maximum return.

In this chapter, we will cover the following topics:

- Financial concepts
- The Markowitz mean-variance model
- The Treynor-Black model
- Portfolio construction using the Treynor-Black model
- Trend prediction

Financial concepts

In this section, we will explore various financial concepts. For an in-depth survey of the domain knowledge, you are encouraged to refer to the syllabus of the **Chartered Finance Analyst (CFA)**.

Alpha and beta returns in the capital asset pricing model

According to the **capital asset pricing model (CAPM)**, investment return equals the *risk-free rate + alpha + beta * market return + noise* (with a mean of zero). Alpha is the return earned by the superior performance of the firm or investors, while beta is the riskiness of the asset in comparison to the overall market return. Beta is high when the risk of the investment is riskier than the average market. Noise is the random movement or luck that has a long-term return of zero.

The asset management industry, especially professional investment managers, is commonly charging clients based on alpha. That explains why people pay so much attention to alpha.

Realized and unrealized investment returns

Investment returns (gain) can be realized or unrealized. Realized return is the return that is actualized and pocketed. Unrealized return is the return we would have pocketed today if we had sold the assets for money.

Investment policy statements

The investment industry works on investing on behalf of the asset owner. As an asset manager, it is our fiduciary duty to advise and invest on behalf of the client. So far in this book, we have tried to understand the investment needs of investors by looking at behavioral/trading data. However, the key data is, in fact, the **investment policy statement (IPS)** that the investors will establish.

An IPS contains the return objective, risk appetite, and constraints laid down by the investor. The return objective and risk appetite are both variables that we can define quantitatively. Return can be defined as the net annual return of the inflation rate. If the target return is 1% and the inflation rate is 1%, then this means the value of capital is preserved as the price level of goods increases by the inflation rate. In the long run, the purchasing power we put into the portfolio remains the same because the value grows in line with the price level.

Each of these variables can be mathematically expressed as follows:

- **Return objective**: This return objective is called capital preservation. The 1% return rate is called the nominal rate of return. After deducting the inflation rate from the nominal rate, it is called the real rate of return:

$$Real\ rate\ of\ return = Nominal\ rate\ of\ return - Inflation\ rate$$

- **Risk appetite**: Risk appetite can be defined as the volatility of a return. We normally define it like this:

$$Risk\ appetite\ of\ an\ investor = Variance\ of\ the\ real\ rate\ of\ return$$

The choice of risk appetite is subjective—some people like the ups and downs that accompany this excitement. While some prefer to read this book while sitting on the sofa (pretty boring, isn't it?), some prefer to read it seated on a chair at the table. Some people prefer to work in a boring 9 to 5 with steady pay, while others prefer the excitement of a start-up, with the hope of getting rich quickly and risking the possibility of failure.

That said, boring does not mean there is a lower risk of being laid off, and an exciting job does not imply a high risk of losing out on the job. There are obvious cases where we have an exciting job, high potential, and stability. That's exactly the target result of asset allocation from this portfolio management process.

Given that this book concerns practical aspects of work, for more details, I recommend *Managing Investment Portfolio, A Dynamic Process* by the CFA Institute (`https://www.wiley.com/en-us/ Managing+Investment+Portfolios%3A+A+Dynamic+Process%2C+3rd+Editi on-p-9780470080146`). Our objective here is to define the necessary parameters to execute the machine learning program in Python.

The challenge, in the age of AI, is how to bring this policy to life in the form of code that a machine would understand. Indeed, the investment community has the task of digitizing investment policy.

Recent advancements in blockchain promise smart contracts, which is based on the assumption that certain statements could be digitized as logic. If a contract could be coded as a smart contract on the blockchain for execution, then why not an IPS? Let's assume that the investment policy is codified for the rest of this chapter.

Asset class

Portfolio management is the process of allocating capital to various investment assets based on the characteristics of the asset class or risk factors. We'll begin by focusing on asset class allocation. An **asset class** is defined as a group of assets that bear similar characteristics. It actually sounds quite similar to the outcome of a clustering model.

To blend in our the knowledge of finance, asset classes normally refer to equity, bonds, the money market, and alternative investments. **Alternative investments** can be subdivided into real estate, private equity, hedge funds, and commodities. **Equity** refers to the equity shares issued in the publicly traded market, while **bonds** refer to the debt issued by companies. The **money market** refers to short-term debt that has a duration of between one day and one year. They are different from bonds as the money market is highly liquid (heavily traded with a fairly priced market), whereas, in bond issues, the market can either be very illiquid or dominated by certain investors. Bonds typically refer to debt that has a longer duration, such as 10 years of maturity or beyond. Of course, it can include anything above 1 year, typically called **notes**.

Players in the investment industry

Investors play a central role in the finance industry. It is, however, equally important to know the other major players—investment managers (who manage the investor's money), brokers who are referred to as the sell side (typically, an investment bank or securities firm), and consultants and advisers who provide specialized advice to investors on how to choose investment managers. Custodians refer to the party that looks after the settlement and the administrative aspects of any investment transactions and filings with the exchange markets.

If the investment managers are from institutions, they are referred to as **institutional investors**, whereas someone who is acting on their own is called an **individual investor**. Institutional investors have fiduciary duties to the beneficiary owners of the investment money. Those beneficiaries are the real customers of the investment managers. For instance, in the case of Duke Energy, the ultimate beneficiaries could be the employees of Duke Energy. In between, it could either be the treasurer who manages the fund as the investment manager, or it could be the outsourced investment fund managers who are the chosen investment managers.

On the sales side of the industry, the fund could be for institutional investors, individual investors, or retail distribution via banks or insurance companies. In the case of retail distribution, the responsibility of fitting the investment to the needs of the owners lies with the distributors. While it is the institutional investors or individual investors that deal directly with the investment managers, it's the investment managers or consultants who are responsible for the matching.

Benchmark – the baseline of comparison

A benchmark is used by the investment portfolio to define what average market return they should be measured against. It could refer to the market return or the beta in the CAPM. Anything above the average is called **alpha**. In this chapter's example, we assume that the global equity **Exchange-Traded Fund** (**ETF**) is the market benchmark.

If we were to construct the world's market benchmark for an investor in the world's assets, we could analytically create such an index that weighted the various indices or baskets of returns.

Investors are return-seeking

A study by the Bank of International Settlement shows that investors are exhibiting return-chasing behavior. This means that one of the key principles of investment is to follow the market (return). It also surely means that we will always be slower than the market if we solely let returns drive our allocation decisions. So, in the world of AI, there could be two ways to improve:

- Being very quick to follow the return trend with a super-fast machine
- Predicting the market better than the crowd

An ETF promises to do the former, provided that we do the allocation to the ETF quickly enough—which, in turn, defeats the purpose of following the markets as there are so many different kinds of ETFs. It is only possible when we invest in a true market representative—for example, a major market index ETF; otherwise, we are still going back to the same challenge of trying to allocate to the right securities/investments to generate alpha (beating the market).

In most trading books, the author will hide what their winning strategies are—which makes our understanding of what a strategy actually is difficult. To remain really practical, we are going to work on a losing strategy, which you can improve on. This, at least, shows you end-to-end strategy development and gives you a full view of how trading works.

Trend following fund

After allocating assets to the fund manager, let's dig deeper into the fund being invested. If we were the ETF, one of our key needs would be to track the underlying securities. For example, if the fund's mandate is to track the performance of a basket of securities given a set of rules, we can just simply buy and hold the underlying assets until redemption (that is, the investors withdraw their money).

However, if we try to predict the pricing movement in advance and act accordingly, there is a chance that we win more than just the benchmark—this is what we refer to as **alpha**.

Using technical analysis as a means to generate alpha

A school of thought in trading believes in the trends exhibited in the pricing of securities. This is called **technical analysis**. It assumes that past pricing movements can predict future movement. The following graph shows the trend in the price of securities over a certain period of time:

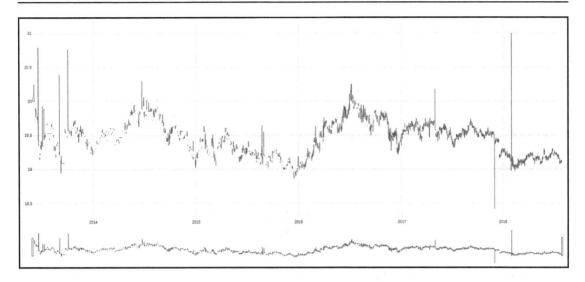

At a very high level, we see that the securities price moves in trend, but the length of the trend is not always the same. There has been a wealth of studies on how to read the patterns seen on the pricing movement across time. But isn't this a computer vision challenge? As opposed to us hand-picking countless numbers of features, should we leave it to a computer to read the graphs and learn how to chart trend lines?

 In terms of types of patterns, a good place to start is *Technical Analysis of the Financial Markets: A Comprehensive Guide to Trading Methods and Applications* (New York Institute of Finance). For information on exact data processing to detect patterns, please refer to *Advances in Machine Learning*. Here, Dr. Prado really takes it to another level by giving you an insight into the working before the data is fed to the machine.

Trading decisions – strategy

A trading strategy refers to the considerations and actions to be taken on trading activities. So, in this chapter, as opposed to barring the strategies, I will show you an actual strategy that failed at its design. For a real trader, disclosing the winning trading strategy will kill the strategy because people can trade against it—for example, an opposing trader can also sell when you are expected to buy and vice versa.

The brief strategy we present here does not generate positive alpha compared to a simple buy-and-hold strategy with the same asset. However, I will indicate ways to improve it.

To learn more about the comparative behaviors of traders and bankers, please refer to *Compensating Financial* Experts by *The Journal of Finance* (`https://onlinelibrary.wiley.com/doi/abs/10.1111/jofi.12372`).

Understanding the Markowitz mean-variance model

The objective of portfolio management is to minimize risk in order to ascertain the target return, given that, for the specific investor, we have the target return and risk tolerance captured from the IPS and historical returns. Typical portfolio optimization models used in the industry include the Markowitz mean-variance model and the Treynor-Black model.

An economist, named Harry Markowitz, introduced mean-variance analysis, which is also known as **Modern Portfolio Theory** (**MPT**), in 1952. He was awarded a Nobel Prize in Economics for his theory.

The mean-variance model is a framework for assembling asset portfolios so that a return can be maximized for a given risk level. It is an extension of investment diversification. **Investment diversification** is an idea that suggests investors should invest in different kinds of financial assets. Investment diversification is less risky in comparison to investing in only one type of asset.

The investors choose the asset allocation that maximizes return, also known as the **variance of return**. While investing in assets, the risk to reward ratio becomes a critical decision-making factor. The risk to reward ratio is calculated as the ratio of expected returns to possible losses. The difference between the expected return and the actual return is known as **risk**. The key challenge is the calculation of the variance of return on the target portfolio. For example, it could be 40% equity and 60% bonds or an even more complex asset class allocation, such as real estate, commodities, and more. To come up with a variance of return with 40% equity and 60% bonds, we need to first calculate the variance of return for equities and bonds separately. At the same time, we also have to consider the covariance between the equity and bond, that is, how the return of equities and bonds goes hand in hand in the same direction or a completely different direction.

For detailed insights into how the asset and wealth management industry is shaping up, please refer to *PwC, 2017, Asset Management 2020: Taking stock, Asset & Wealth Management Insights.*

Imagine a team of people (where each person represents one asset class) working together on a task to deliver a return. The work of a portfolio manager is to determine who has more say and who has less say within the group (asset allocation work). This depends on the productivity (return) and fluctuation of the person's performance: some people exhibit extreme levels of performance, while some are pretty stable in terms of their productivity (variance). We also need to know the interaction between individual team members—this interaction also has to consider how each of them complements or amplifies each other's productivity (correlation). Some team members show strong chemistry between two of them to deliver extremely good results (positive correlation), some work at different times of the day—one is a night owl and the other a morning person—each with different productive hours (negative correlation), and some don't really have any consistent pattern of similarity or dissimilarity (zero correlation).

The following diagram shows the correlation matrix between two assets (**i** and **j**). The diagonal line in gray shows the securities' return variance and the remaining cells show inter-security return covariance. The cells in black are not needed, as they mirror the values opposite to the diagonal line. For a mere 20 securities, we will have 190 values to be estimated:

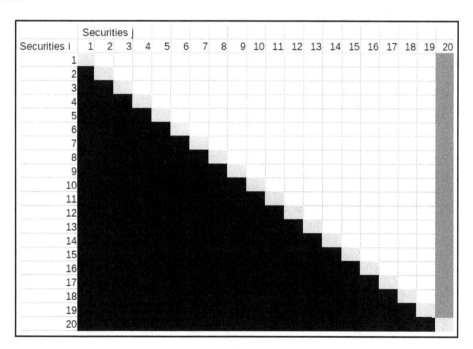

To illustrate this problem further, let's assume that security **20** is not liquid, and we cannot reliably estimate its covariance with another security. We could have impacted the data quality of covariance with the other 19 securities. The problem with this model in a real-life application is as follows:

- Some assets do not have enough data points for us to calculate their correlation with others (for example, new team members to the team).
- In financial markets, the correlation between assets changes dynamically, and it is hard to forecast a forward-looking correlation.
- The correlation is not linear.

This model works on public equity with efficient pricing and lots of data points for modeling. But it does not work on non-liquid assets—such as private equity in start-ups or emerging market securities or bonds, where we don't have full visibility of the pricing and many are often reconstructed analytically.

 One specific type of correlation in risk could be credit risk—in good times, the correlation of risk across assets is low; whereas, in crisis, the correlation spikes and moves in a similar direction. Please refer to *Credit Risk Pricing, Measurement and Management,* by Duffie D. and Singleton, K.J., for an example on default correlation.

Some treasurers in established firms are responsible for managing their own pension money. We assume that treasurers need to handle the target asset allocation for the pension fund. We will take the index return data for each of the asset classes. We will use Quandl's subscribed data on the ETF as the data source.

An ETF refers to funds that can be bought and sold on a public exchange such as the **New York Stock Exchange** (**NYSE**). It is a fund because it invests in many more underlying securities such as stocks or bonds. It is becoming more popular as it allows investors to focus on the themes that the funds are investing in, rather than individual stocks. For example, we can have a strong view about the strength of the US economy by buying the fund that invests in the largest 500 stocks of the US.

Exploring the Treynor-Black model

Due to the instability of the Markowitz mean-variance model in managing problems associated with multi-asset class portfolios, the Treynor-Black model was established. Treynor-Black's model fits the modern portfolio allocation approach where there are certain portfolios that are active and others that are passive. Here, passive refers to an investment that follows the market rate of return—not to beat the market average return but to closely follow the market return.

An active portfolio refers to the portfolio of investment in which we seek to deliver an above-market average return. The lower the market return with a market risk level, the higher the portfolio. Then, we allocate the total capital to an active portfolio. So, why take more risk if the market return is good enough? The Treynor-Black model seeks to allocate more weight to the asset that delivers a higher return/risk level out of the total risk/return level of the active portfolio.

Introducing ResNet – the convolutional neural network for pattern recognition

What is specific about applying the computer vision type of neural network is that we can use the following hidden layers. In our example, we will use ResNet implemented in Keras as an example to illustrate these ideas. We will also showcase an approach to improve performance—however, you are expected to dig deeper into hyperparameter tuning.

The convolutional layer is like taking a subset of the image that is being inputted. In technical analysis, it's like having a sliding window to calculate a statistical value. Each type of sliding window is trained to detect a certain pattern such as upward, downward, and flat lines. In neural network terminology, each type is called a **filter**. For each type of filter, there are numbers of windows to fully run (or slide) through the input image; the number is represented by the number of neurons in the layer.

To explain the terminology, let's take an input image of size *3 × 3* and a kernel shape of *2 × 2*. Our actual input in the coding example is larger than this size.

The **input image** is a *3 × 3* image with a black line (represented by 3 pixels) crossing from the bottom-left corner to the upper-right corner diagonally. It shows a stock price that is moving upward by one pixel every day:

The shape of the sliding windows is called a **kernel**. A kernel is a function that can transform an inputted matrix/vector into another form, as shown in the following diagram:

For illustration, we assume the kernel size to be 2 × 2, *stride = 1*, and zero padding unless specified.

The numbers in the following diagram show the sequence of the kernel movement. Each movement will be represented by one neuron at the convolution layer:

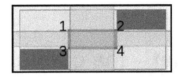

The following diagram shows the 2 × 2 kernel, and the kernel moves 4 times (that is, 4 neurons are required):

- **Kernel shape**: As the kernel moves (we call it slides), it may or may not cover the same input pixel, which makes the blue darker as we want to show which pixels are covered more than once:

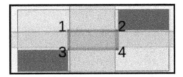

The kernel *shape = 2 × 2*, and it takes 4 moves to cover the full image:

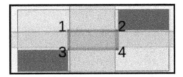

The kernel *shape = 1 × 1*, and it takes 9 moves to cover the full image.

- **Stride**: This shows how many pixels need to be moved toward the right and downward as it advances:

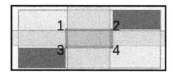

Here, *stride = 1,* and it takes 4 moves to cover the image. Note that every time there will be overlapping pixels covered:

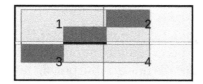

Here, *stride = 2,* and it takes 4 moves to cover the image. Note that every time there will not be any overlapping pixels covered by the filter.

- **Padding**: This shows how many white pixels are surrounding the inputted image:

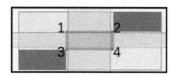

The following diagram shows zero padding:

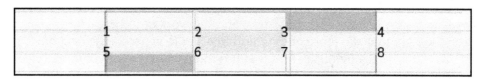

Here, *padding = 1,* which allows the edge cell on the side to be covered by a different neuron.

Pooling layer

The pooling layer is quite self-explanatory—it is meant for pooling the results from the input. Imagine that after the convolutional layer, for each type of filter, there will be a number of outputs—for example, four. Can we reduce this to one variable instead of four output variables? Pooling can play the role of compressing this information. For example, taking the maximum of the four outputs (max pooling) or averaging the four outputs (average pooling). Visually, the meaning of the pooling layer is to blur the image or calculate moving average trends.

ReLU activation layer

For finance professionals, the **Rectifier Linear Unit (ReLU)** layer is like a call option payoff—once a certain threshold is exceeded, the output value is changed linearly with the input. Its significance is to reduce the noise in the pricing to ensure that only a strong market trend is considered.

Softmax

Softmax is a super-charged version of the logistics regression model that we touched on in the earlier chapters of this book with multiple predicted outcomes—for example, the version one binary outcome in the logistics regression model case. In our case, we wish to identify what the pricing would be on the next day.

Portfolio construction using the Treynor-Black model

Let's say we are given 10 days of pricing data, and the work of technical analysis is to draw the lines on the right to make sense of the trend in order to generate the next day's pricing for the 11th day. It is quite obvious to find that it is indeed what a convolutional neural network could tackle.

Knowing that, practically, the time unit we are looking at could be per 100 ms or 10 ms instead of 1 day, but the principle will be the same:

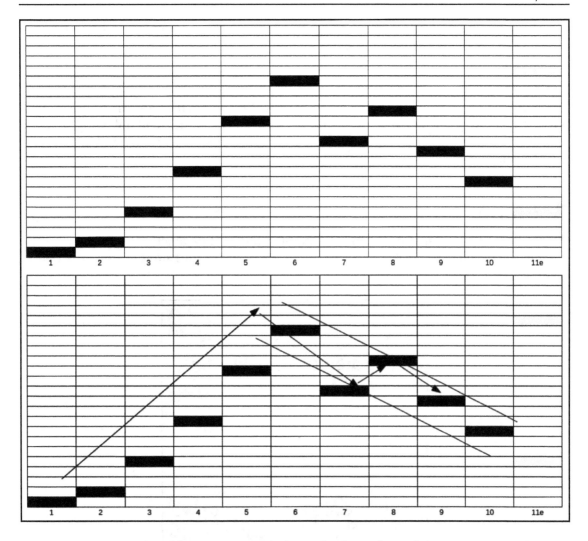

Let's continue with the Duke Energy example. In this hypothetical case, we assume that we are the treasurer running the pension fund plan of Duke Energy with a total asset size of 15 billion USD with a defined contribution plan. Presumably, we know what our IPS is in digital format:

- Target return = 5% of real return (that means deducting the inflation of goods)
- Risk = return volatility equals 10%
- Constraints: No electricity utility companies to avoid investing in other peers/competitors

Please note that this is a hypothetical example. No inference will be made about the actual company.

Using the IPS, we will first illustrate how to allocate the fund to the various asset classes as the first example. Then, in the second example, we will look at the trend following strategy to enable the investment managers to follow the market, given the recent trend in passive investment.

Solution

We have created two separate Python files because the asset parameters should be independent of how the asset is allocated. There are a total of four steps for this. The two main steps (the files) are as follows:

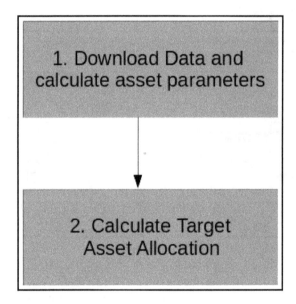

We will download and estimate the asset parameters and generate the target asset allocation:

1. To download and estimate the asset parameters, we will import libraries and key variable values. Then, we will define functions to download data for each of the assets, the market return, the risk-free rate, the asset return, and the parameters.

2. To generate the target asset allocation, we will import libraries and key variable values, find out the weight of the securities in the active portfolio, and find out the weight of the active portfolio in the total portfolio.

 As we progress through the chapters, we will try to illustrate the use of traditional databases via this example, rather than creating a data dump without database storage. It follows our point made earlier that a structured database (a SQL database) works perfectly with securities' pricing data where the data is structured. We are using SQLite, which is a lighter version of the database. It is only meant to illustrate to the finance professional how databases come into play in our use case. For actual IT implementation, of course, we can use a lot of enterprise-grade databases that are both secure and fast.

Downloading price data on an asset in scope

Individual assets and market assets used in this example are all ETFs. Data is downloaded from Quandl using free and paid subscriptions—including the risk-free data represented by the US treasury notes and the market return represented by the global equity ETF. After we download the data, which is the end-of-day data, we also need to define what we refer to as the price. In our example, we take the middle point between the daily high and the daily low as the price for the day.

The steps are as follows:

1. Import the necessary libraries; `sqlite3` is newly introduced in this chapter. This shows how the SQL database could be used for trading data use cases. We will use a lightweight SQL database, called **SQLite**, which itself is shown as a file:

6A_1_cal_assetpara.py

```
'''****************************************
#1. Import libraries and key variable values
'''
import quandl
import pandas as pd
import numpy as np
from sklearn import linear_model
from sklearn.metrics import r2_score
import sqlite3
import math
import os
#not needed when using database
import pickle
```

```
#API Key

#dates variables for all the download

#db file
```

2. Define the function to download data for each of the assets:

```
'''****************************************
#2. Define function to download data for each of the asset
'''
```

 Without Python, you can also directly assess the file via a tool, such as a plugin to the Chrome browser, SQLite viewer and more.

The function will download the price data of any given ticker in the SHARADAR database from Quandl. In addition to this, it will calculate the return of the ticket on a daily basis.

What it does is download the data and then calculate the return series.

Calculating the risk-free rate and defining the market

In our example, we take the US 3-month treasury notes as the proxy for a risk-free rate of return. In the investment world, the US is considered risk-free and the government will never default. Any return we earn above the risk-free rate is the return we get by taking more risk.

The market, as a whole, can be represented by the return from all of the investment assets around the world—this is easy in theory, but in reality, it is really hard to define. The most challenging part is generating this market return on a regular basis so that it could be used in the next step. We will take a shortcut and use an ETF to represent the market return:

```
'''****************************************
#3. Market Return
'''
```

Given a ticker as the market proxy, run the preceding function:

```
'''****************************************
#4. Risk Free Rate
'''
#day count
```

```
#risk free rate

# override return of market
```

The risk-free rate is rather complex. By convention, the industry uses a 3-month treasury note. To obtain the risk-free rate for the whole period, we take around 10 years of data to calculate the risk-free rate for the period.

However, we also need to annualize the interest rate. By definition of a 3-month treasury note, the number of days counted is 360 days. The interest rate is where every day is counted.

Calculating the alpha, beta, and variance of error of each asset type

After understanding what the risk-free return rate and market return are, our next task is to find out the alpha, beta, and variance of error by regressing the market return against the asset's return:

Investment Return = Risk-Free Rate + Alpha + Beta * market return + noise (Variance of error)

After performing this calculation, we will keep the data in a SQLite database for retrieval later on.

I believe, in the future of start-ups, our robo-advisor will be focusing on ETF/smart beta—that is, the allocation of sectors to generate a return against the market. Therefore, in this example, I choose the ETF tickers.

We will run a linear regression of the sector ETF against the market benchmark. However, the day in which we can have a price quotation of the ETF and the market could be different; therefore, we will regress only when both the sector ETF and market ETF have a price—using the inner join command on SQL.

Inner join implicitly requires that the index of both the sector ETF and the market benchmark have to be the same before joining. The index of the dataset refers to the date of return:

```
'''*************************************
#5. Asset Return and parameters
'''
#list of stocks for selection in the active portfolio

#connect to the databases and reset it everytime with drop indicator
```

```
#write out the risk free and market parameters

#loop through the tickers
for tkr in list_tkr:
 #calculate the CAPM:
 #download data for the ticker

#make sure the ticket we select has market data

 #linear regression

#obtain the result and write out the parameters
```

Calculating the optimal portfolio allocation

We are at the second major process—that is, working out the portfolio allocation. First, we will calculate the active portfolio size and weight of different asset within the active portfolio. The steps are as follows:

1. Import all of the relevant libraries:

   6A_2_treynor_black.py

   ```
   '''*************************************
   #1. Import libraries and key variable values
   '''
   import sqlite3
   import datetime

   #create a table to store weight
   ```

2. Calculate the active portfolio's parameters and compare them against the market performance to find out how much weight from the total portfolio we should allocate to the active portfolio:

   ```
   '''*************************************
   #2. Find out the weight of the securities in the active portfolio
   '''
   #total alpha/variance of the active securities

   #insert into the table the weight of each active securities
   ```

   The weight of the active portfolio is solved by aggregating the parameters for the securities (sector ETF) that belong to the active portfolio.

3. Then, based on the ratio of the market return/risk, as compared to the active portfolio return/risk, the stronger the active portfolio performs, the more weight it gets out of the total portfolio:

```
'''*************************************
#3. Find out the weight of the active portfolio in the total
portfolio
'''
#calculate the parameters of the active portfolio

#read back the risk free and market para

#calculate the weight of active portfolio

#display the result
```

After the optimal portfolio is obtained, the next step is to allocate it to *you* according to the IPS on return and risk.

The following two constraints need to be satisfied:

- *% Optimal portfolio x Return by Optimal portfolio + (1-%Optimal portfolio) x Return by risk-free asset >= Return required by IPS*
- *% Optimal portfolio x Risk by Optimal portfolio <= Risk required by IPS*

Congratulations! You have learned how to allow capital to different investment assets to yield the optimal return and risk level. In the next section, we will look at an example on how to predict the trend of a security. This will help investors to make wise investment decisions.

Predicting the trend of a security

In the preceding example, we played the role of a trader who followed the portfolio allocation set by the treasurer. Assuming that our job is to follow the securities required by the treasurer, the profit and loss of the trader hinges on how can we profit from buying low and selling high. We took the daily pricing history of securities as the data to build our model. In the following section, we will demonstrate how to predict the trend before making buy decisions for assets.

Solution

There are two major processes—one on model development and another on model backtesting. Both processes include a total of eight steps for real-time deployment, which we will not include here. However, it is very similar to model backtesting. The following diagram illustrates the flow of the process:

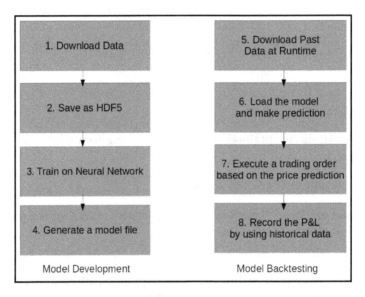

Loading, converting, and storing data

In this step, we will load the data, convert the data into an image array, and then store it in a HDF5 data file format. First, we will load the data from Quandl as a data frame, and then convert the data into an array—which will plot the data like it was presented earlier. In our example, we simplify the problem by plotting only day end data points for one day. We only take the middle point of the day high and the day low, without considering its transaction volume.

When it comes to plotting the price on an array with fixed dimensions, on the y axis—the price—we will develop a function to fix the maximum and minimum values into the fixed dimension by scaling the data points in between the maximum and minimum accordingly. This is called **normalization**. On the x axis, each day is represented by one point on the x axis, where the far left is the earliest day and the far right is the latest day of a given window size. On a given point, the color of the price point is of the same, *color = 255* for showing it in pictures, or 1 for feeding it to neural network.

The same treatment is done on the target variable—which is only the next day chart using the same scale for y. If the next day is actually higher than the maximum or lower than the minimum, we can force it to take the current maximum and minimum point.

After the array is prepared, we will then stack up the array for the duration specified—with every single day represented by one chart that shows the past X days, with X being the window size. When we have finished stacking up, we will put the whole array into a HDF5 file—this is a distributed file format in nature, and it allows the file to be stored across multiple physical locations.

Define the libraries and variables. We have a defined a list of tickers to go through for the download step:

6B_1_trendFollowing.py

```
'''*************************************
#1. Import libraries and key variable values

'''
import quandl
import plotly
import plotly.graph_objs as go
import numpy as np

from datetime import datetime
try:
    import Image
except ImportError:
    from PIL import Image
import os
import h5py

#dates parameters
...
#quandl setting
...
#parameters for the image generation
...
#create path for the output dataset
...
#ticker lists
...
#generate png file for each of the input or now
...
#generate interactive plot to the ticket stock price or not
...
```

Define the function to put the stock price of variable range into a fixed-sized image of fixed height and width. It will return a column of values that has been rescaled along with the scaling factor:

- *Pixel value = (price value – minimum value of the column) x number of pixels per value*
- *Number of pixels = (maximum value of the column - minimum value of the column) / total number of pixels*

The code is as follows:

```
'''*****************************************
#2. Define the function to rescale the stock price according to the min and
max values

'''
#input_X is a series of price
#output_X is a series of price expressed in pixel
def rescale(input_X, pixel, min_x,max_x):
...
```

Ticker by ticker, we will download and convert the data into an input image and target result for machine learning as the next step. The most technical aspect of these codes relates to HDF5 file saving. Within the file, it is further divided into a dataset, and, within the dataset, we can store the files inside. One specific feature of dataset is that its size is fixed once it is defined at creation. Additionally, it is not meant to be dynamically updated—though, this is technically possible.

Colored images are stored in three channels—red, green, and blue—each channel is a matrix where each pixel ranges from the value of 0 to 255. However, in our example, we will only use one channel for black and white pictures. Before we store the image to HDF5, all the numbers are divided by 255 so that the input variables are in a range between 0 and 1 for neural network training later.

To give you a real feeling of the data, we also have another interactive chart feature (using `ploty`) provided. This was also turned off to improve speed. However, for a first-time user of the code, it is recommended that you try it out to see the data being downloaded.

Please refer to image processing texts for an in-depth discussion—my favorite is *Feature Extraction & Image Processing for Computer Vision* by Nixon M.S. and Aguado, A.S., as it focuses a lot on extracting features that we need as opposed to just laying out the theoretical background.

However, the downside is that this book's code is not in Python—which is an acceptable challenge given that learning the principle is more important than code that evolves:

```
'''***************************************
#3. Go through the tickers
'''
for tkr in tkr_list:
    ...
    #if the ticker has been downloaded, skip the ticket and go for the next
      one
    ...
    #download and create dataset
    ...
    #sort the date from ascending to descending...
    ...
    #charting interactive chart for viewing the data
    ...
    #calculate mid price of the day
    ...
    #remove the file if there is one
    ...
    #remove the file if there is one
    ...
    #create dataset within the HDF5 file
    #now we create the dataset with a fixed size to fit all the data, it
      could also be create to fit fixed batches
    ...
    #loop through the dates
    for i in range(num_img):
        ...
        #create min and max values for the mid price plot within a given
          timeframe
        ...
        #in case of low liquidity ETF which has the same price, no graph be
          drawn
        ...
        #draw the dot on the x, y axis of the input image array
        ...
        #output the image for visualization
        ...
        #draw the dot on the target image for training
        ...
        #stack up for a numpy for Image Recognition
        ...
```

Setting up the neural network

Following the code from the Keras examples in regard to ResNet, we do not perform any alternation of the network design. We take both version 1 and version 2 while disabling the batch normalization, given that the data point has the same color, and the y axis is normalized for a given window size, so there is not much significance in further normalizing it.

 Batch normalization has to do with harmonizing the values seen in the network in the current batch of records—it works well if the color we plot on an image contains different colors. However, since we have already normalized the pricing at each data point on its y axis, the codes are unchanged for now as we need this when we feed in data with different scales and distributions.

Loading the data to the neural network for training

We retrieved the data from the HDF5 file earlier and put it in the network that was just set up in the previous step. There will be a splitting of the training, testing and validation sets. However, in our case, we just take all of the data as the training and testing sets at the same time. The validation set can be another stock—given that we are training only the general intelligence to observe the technical movement of stock.

We feed the network with batch normalization and a certain epoch number. This step takes the most time.

During training, we keep a log of the performance for visualization later:

6B_2_TrainCNN.py

```
'''***********************************
#1. Import libraries and key variable values
'''
'''***********************************
#2. Define functions
'''
def lr_schedule(epoch):
def resnet_layer(inputs,
                num_filters=16,
                kernel_size=3,
                strides=1,
                activation='relu',
                batch_normalization=True,
                conv_first=True):
```

```
def resnet_v1(input_shape, depth, num_classes=10):
def resnet_v2(input_shape, depth, num_classes=10):
```

 Please refer to https://arxiv.org/abs/1512.03385 for an explanation on the design, and refer to the Keras documentation for further implementation details: https://keras.io/applications/#resnet50.

What the code essentially does is to create two different neural network designs of different structures—given that we have a sizable data input with the data source, readers will experience a better performance with version 2 as long as the data is sizable:

```
#3. Execute the model training
'''
# Computed depth from supplied model parameter n

# Model name, depth and version

# create list of batches to shuffle the data

#check if the prev step is completed before starting

#decide if we should load a model or not

#loop through the tickers

#load dataset saved in the previous preparation step

#start if both file exists:

#calculate number of batches
 #do it at the first one

# Input image dimensions.
        # Prepare model model saving directory.

        # Prepare callbacks for model saving and for learning rate
          adjustment

        # loop over batches

            # Run training, without data augmentation.

        #when model training finished for the ticket, create a file to
          indicate its completion

# Score trained model.
```

Saving and fine-tuning the neural network

The network is saved at the end. We did not fine-tune our model at all in this example—but it has to do with hyperparameters tuning—which means that we should tune every single parameter in the network so far. I would recommend that you look at *Machine Learning Yearning* by Andrew Ng (https://www.deeplearning.ai/machine-learning-yearning/). This step is not implemented in this example. But we have illustrated it in more detail in Chapter 3, *Using Features and Reinforcement Learning to Automate Bank Financing*.

Loading the runtime data and running through the neural network

The network can be loaded again and run on a new dataset as a validation set. However, in our example, we take another stock to test whether this generic technical analysis machine works or not. The output of the network is the prediction of the next day's pricing.

In this program, the most special data will be the strategy parameters. It all starts with one monetary value. And we are testing three strategies—one buy and hold, which is the benchmark, and two takes on different pricing outputs to trade.

The steps involved are as follows:

1. Import all the necessary libraries and variables:

    ```
    6B_3_RunCNN.py
    ```

    ```
    '''***************************************
    #1. Import libraries and key variable values
    '''
    #folder path

    #date range for full dataset

    #Create list of dates

    #API key for quandl

    #Parameters for the image generation

    #model path

    #number of channel for the image

    #strategies parameter
    ```

With ResNet v2, we have close to 1 million parameters, while we are feeding roughly 3 millions of records ~14.5 years x 200 trading days x 125 tickers (but some tickers are not liquid to trade).

2. Then, define the functions to fit the price points into the image with a fixed height:

```
'''**************************************
#2. Define functions
'''
```

3. Get new data and run the functions to predict the price. Load data from a ticket and prepare the data; then, run the model built from the training process:

```
'''**************************************
#3. Running the test
'''
#Get the data

#write header for the log of the strategy back-testing

#loop through the dates
  #make sure both start and end dates are valid

#prepare the input data

#if no trend, then drop this data point

#stack up for a numpy for Image Recognition
  #print the historical data

#make prediction
#Obtain predicted price
```

Generating a trading strategy from the result and performing performance analysis

For a given price prediction, we can devise different actions to do with the price prediction.

The objective of this loop is to measure the profit and loss of the trading strategies by relying on the prediction made by the model in the previous section.

At any given date, there will be only one price prediction, in the form of a 1D array with the probability at each price point given the scale. The various strategies (1 and 2) handle what to do with the prediction:

```
#calculate expected values

#Strategy Back-Testing
 #Benchmark - Strategy 0 - buy and hold

#Testing of strategy1

#Testing of strategy2

#print the final result of the strategies
```

Congratulations! You have walked through the process of price prediction using computer vision models.

In the real world, there could be more predictions made by different models, which will add complexity to the number of strategies tested. We require a benchmark to know whether these strategies outperform the normal market situation, which are buy and hold strategies. If our strategies are successful, then they should be able to outperform the market by showing higher profit and loss figures.

In strategy backtesting, we normally deploy it to an out-of-time, unseen sample.

Summary

In this chapter, we learned a number of portfolio management techniques. We combined them with AI to automate the decision-making process when buying assets. We learned about the Markowitz mean-variance model and the Treynor-Black model for portfolio construction. We also looked at an example of portfolio construction using the Treynor-Black model. We also learned how to predict trends in the trading of a security.

In the next chapter, we will look at the sell side of asset management. We will learn about sentiment analysis, algorithmic marketing for investment products, network analysis, and how to extract network relationships. We will also explore techniques such as Network X and tools such as Neo4j and PDF Miner.

7
Sensing Market Sentiment for Algorithmic Marketing at Sell Side

In the previous chapter, we learned about investment portfolio management. We also learned some of the portfolio management techniques, such as the Markowitz mean-variance model and the Treynor–Black model for portfolio construction. We also learned about how to predict a trend for a security. So, the previous chapter was based on the buy side of a market. It depicted the behavior of portfolio managers or asset managers.

In this chapter, we will look at the sell side of the market. We will understand the behavior of the counterpart of the portfolio managers. Sell side refers to securities firms/investment banks and their main services, including sales, trading, and research. Sales refers to the marketing of securities to inform investors about the securities available for selling. Trading refers to the services that investors use to buy and sell off securities and the research performed to assist investors in evaluating securities. Being client-centric, one of the key functions of a bank is sensing the needs and sentiments of the end investors, who in turn push the asset managers to buy the product from banks. We will begin this chapter by looking at a few concepts and techniques. We will look at an example that illustrates how to sense the needs of an investor. We will look at another example to analyze the annual report and extract information from it.

The following topics will be covered in this chapter:

- Understanding sentiment analysis
- Sensing market requirements using sentiment analysis
- Network building and analysis using Neo4j

Understanding sentiment analysis

Sentiment analysis is a technique in which text mining is done for contextual information. The contextual information is identified and extracted from the source material. It helps businesses understand the sentiment for their products, securities, or assets. It can be very effective to use the advanced techniques of artificial intelligence for in-depth research in the area of text analysis. It is important to classify the transactions around the following concepts:

- The aspect of security the buyers and sellers care about
- Customers' intentions and reactions concerning the securities

Sentiment analysis is known to be the most common text analysis and classification tool. It receives an incoming message or transaction and classifies it depending on whether the sentiment associated with the transaction is positive, negative, or neutral. By using the sentiment analysis technique, it is possible to input a sentence and understand the sentiment behind the sentence.

Now that we have understood what sentiment analysis is, let's find out how to sense market requirements in the following section.

Sensing market requirements using sentiment analysis

One of the key requirements of a security firm/investment bank on the sell side is to manufacture the relevant securities for the market. We have explored the fundamental behaviors and responsibilities of companies in Chapter 4, *Mechanizing Capital Market Decisions*, and Chapter 5, *Predicting the Future of Investment Bankers*. We learned about the momentum approach in Chapter 6, *Automated Portfolio Management Using the Treynor–Black Model and ResNet*. While the market does not always act rationally, it could be interesting to hear about the market's feelings. That is what we will be doing in this chapter.

In this example, we will be playing the role of the salesperson of an investment bank on the trading floor, trading in equities. What we want to find out is the likes and dislikes regarding securities so that they can market the relevant securities, including derivatives. We got our insights from Twitter Search, and the stock price from Quandl. All of this data requires a paid license.

Solution and steps

There are a total of three major steps to get the market sentiment using coding implementation. The data is used as shown in the following diagram:

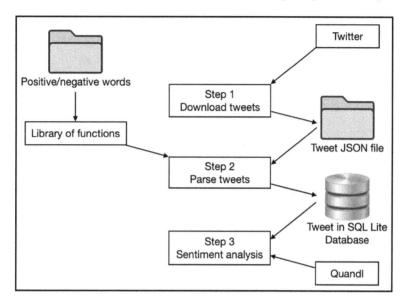

The steps are as follows:

1. Data will be retrieved from Twitter and be saved locally as a JSON file.
2. The JSON file will then be read, further processed by counting the positive and negative words, and input as records into a SQL Lite database.
3. Lastly, the sentiment will be read from the database and compared against stock prices retrieved from Quandl.

We will elaborate on these steps in more detail in the following sections.

Downloading the data from Twitter

By using a Twitter Search commercial license, we download data on the same industry as defined by the Shalender (Quandl) industry classification. We will use the API key to search and download the latest 500 tweets containing or tagged with the company name, one by one. All tweets are received in JSON format, which looks like a Python dictionary. The JSON file will then be saved on the computer for further processing.

Sample Python codes can be found on GitHub (`https://github.com/twitterdev/search-tweets-python`), especially regarding authentication. The following is the code snippet for downloading tweets from Twitter:

```
'''*************************************
#1. Import libraries and key variable values

'''
from searchtweets import ResultStream, gen_rule_payload, load_credentials
from searchtweets import collect_results
import json
import os

script_dir = os.path.dirname(__file__)
#Twitter search commerical accounts credential
premium_search_args = load_credentials("~/.twitter_keys.yaml",
                                       env_overwrite=False)

MAX_RESULTS=500 #maximum at 500

#list of companies in the same industry
...

'''*************************************
#2. download tweets of each company

'''
for comp in comp_list:
    ...
```

Converting the downloaded tweets into records

The tweet's message and any linked page will then be loaded and read by a simple language processing program, which will count the number of positive and negative words in the message and linked page body. The parsed tweet will be converted to a structured SQL database format and stored in a SQL Lite database.

The following is the code snippet to convert tweets into records:

```
'''*************************************
#1. Import libraries and key variable values

'''
import json
import os
import re
import sqlite3
```

```
import 7A_lib_cnt_sentiment as sentiment

#db file
db_path = 'parsed_tweets.db'
db_name = 'tweet_db'

#sql db
...
#load tweet json
...
#loop through the tweets
    ...
    for tweet in data:
        ...
        tweet_txt_pos,tweet_txt_neg = sentiment.cnt_sentiment(tweet_txt)
        keywords,sentences_list,words_list = \
                                        sentiment.NER_topics(tweet_txt)
        ...
        if len(url_link)>0:
            ...
            url_txt = sentiment.url_to_string(url)
            temp_tweet_link_txt_pos, temp_tweet_link_txt_neg = \
                                        sentiment.cnt_sentiment(url_txt)
            link_keywords,link_sentences_list,link_words_list = \
                                        sentiment.NER_topics(tweet_txt)
            ...
```

There are three functions that are called by the preceding program. One is used to count the positive and negative words, one looks at the topic concerned, and one retrieves the text in the URL given in the tweet.

The following code snippet defines the functions used in the program:

```
import os
import requests
from bs4 import BeautifulSoup
import re
import spacy
import en_core_web_sm
nlp = en_core_web_sm.load()

...
#cal the positive and negative sentiment words given the text
def cnt_sentiment(text_to_be_parsed):
    ...

def noun_phrase(sentence,item_list,lower):
    ...
```

```
#NER
import spacy
from spacy import displacy
from collections import Counter
import math

#text has to be less than 1000000
def NER_topics(text_to_be_parsed):
    ...
    MAX_SIZE =100000
    ...
    for nlp_cnt in range(number_nlp):
        start_pos = nlp_cnt*MAX_SIZE
        end_pos = min(MAX_SIZE,txt_len-start_pos)+start_pos-1
        txt_selected = text_to_be_parsed[start_pos:end_pos]
        ...
        sentences_list = [x for x in article.sents]
        full_sentences_list+=sentences_list
        for sent in sentences_list:
            phrases_list =[]
            phases_list,items_list = noun_phrase(sent, items_list, \
                                                 lower=True)
    ...

#convert the URL's content into string
def url_to_string(url):
    ...
```

Performing sentiment analysis

The database that stored the parsed tweet will be read by another program. For each record, the sentiment will be represented by aggregate sentiment on a daily basis. Each tweet's sentiment is calculated as the total number of negative sentiments subtracted from positive sentiments. The range of this sentiment score should be in the range of -1 to +1, with -1 representing a totally negative score and +1 a totally positive score. Each day's sentiment score is calculated as the average of all the tweets' sentiment scores for the security. Sentiment scores of all securities in the same industry are plotted on a graph, similar to the following:

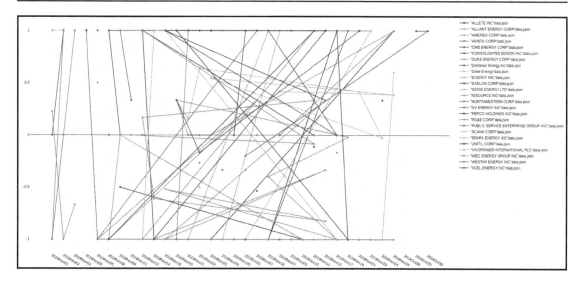

For example, in the short period of our coverage, Dominion Energy has one of the most favorable sentiment scores (between Oct 29 and Oct 30).

The sample output of Dominion Energy is shown in the following graph:

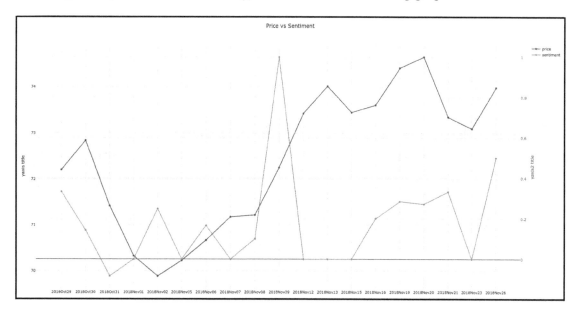

The sentiment is the orange line and the price is the blue line (please refer to the color graph provided in the graphic bundle of this book).

The following is the code snippet for sentiment analysis:

```
'''****************************************
#1. Import libraries and key variable values

'''
import sqlite3
import pandas as pd
import plotly
import plotly.graph_objs as go
import quandl
import json

# Create your connection.
db_path = 'parsed_tweets.db'
cnx = sqlite3.connect(db_path)
db_name = 'tweet_db'

'''****************************************
#2. Gauge the sentiment of each security

'''
...
sql_str = ...
...
print('Sentiment across securities')
field_list = ['positive','negative']
for sec in sec_list:
    ...
```

Comparing the daily sentiment against the daily price

After we obtain the sentiment score for each stock, we also want to know the predictive power or the influence of the sentiment on the stock price. The stock price of the day is calculated by the middle-of-day high and low. For each stock, we plot and compare the sentiment and stock price over a period of time. The following screenshot is an illustration of PG&E Corp's sentiment versus stock price:

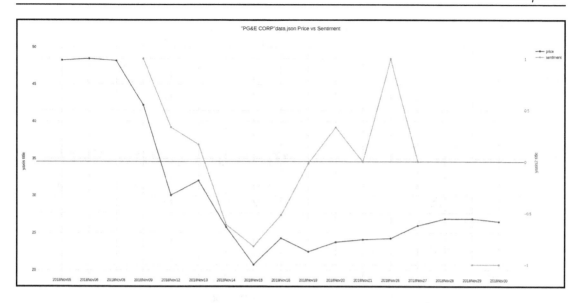

The following is the code snippet for daily sentiment analysis data against the daily price:

```
#run it on different companies
print('Retrieve data')
df_comp = pd.read_csv('ticker_companyname.csv')
corr_results={}

for index, row in df_comp.iterrows():
    tkr = row['ticker']
    name = row['name']

    target_sec = '"'+name +'"data.json'
    corr_result = price_sentiment(tkr,target_sec,date_range)
    try:
        corr_results[name]=corr_result['close'][0]
    except Exception:
        continue

f_corr = open('corr_results.json','w')
json.dump(corr_results,f_corr)
f_corr.close()
```

Congratulations! You have developed a program to assist sales in finding popular securities to develop products for.

From what we have seen, comparing this example to the technical analysis examples, we can see that the information from the sentiment is far higher than the technical trend. So far, we have only looked at the primary impact of the trend, fundamental, and sentiment; however, companies are interconnected in our society. So how can we model the linkage of firms and individuals? This brings us to the next topic—network analysis.

Network building and analysis using Neo4j

As sell-side analysts, besides finding out the primary impact of news on the company, we should also find out the secondary effect of any news. In our example, we will find out the suppliers, customers, and competitors of any news on the stocks.

We can do this using three approaches:

- By means of direct disclosure, such as annual reports
- By means of secondary sources (media reporting)
- By means of industry inferences (for example, raw materials industries, such as oil industries, provide the output for transportation industries)

In this book, we use direct disclosure from the company to illustrate the point.

We are playing the role of equity researchers for the company stock, and one of our key roles is to understand the relevant parties' connections to the company. We seek to find out the related parties of the company—Duke Energy—by reading the company's annual report.

Solution

There are a total of four steps. The following diagram shows the data flow:

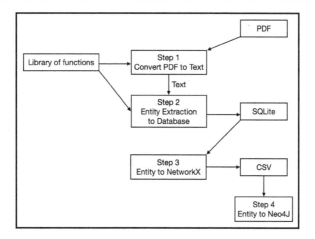

We will now look at the steps in more detail in the following sections.

Using PDFMiner to extract text from a PDF

Besides storage, we also need to extract the relationship from text documents. Before we can start dealing with text, we need to convert the PDF data to text. To do this, we use a library called **PDFMiner** (specifically, the module is called **pdfminer.six** (https://github.com/pdfminer/pdfminer.six) for Python 3+). PDF is an open standard to describe a document. It stores the lines, text, images, and their exact locations in the document. We will only be using a basic function in PDFMiner to extract the texts from it. Even though we could extract the coordinates, we will skip this to simplify our work. Upon extracting the text, we append all lines into one super long line.

The following code snippet imports the necessary libraries and initializes a PDF file to be processed:

```
'''***************************************
#1. Import relevant libraries and variables

'''
#custom made function
import 7B_lib_entitiesExtraction as entitiesExtraction
import 7B_lib_parser_pdf as pdf_parser
import json
import sqlite3

pdf_path = 'annualrpt/NYSE_DUK_2017.pdf'
...
```

Entity extractions

We deploy a linguistic analysis approach called **part-of-speech** (**POS**) tagging to decide whether words X and Z are a company or person, and whether Y is a product or service. Because of the sentence structure, we know that these are nouns, not because we know what X, Y, and Z are.

However, it is still not enough to label the entity. An entity is a standalone subject or object. Since there are too many entities, we should only tag entities with an uppercase first letter as those unique organizations or assets that are pertinent to our work.

The types of entity include ORG, PERSON, FAC, NORP, GPE, LOC, and PRODUCT—that is, Organization, Person, Facilities, Nationalities or religious or political groups, Geo-spatial, Location, and Product, using the SpaCy model.

Upon getting the text chunk from the PDF of step 1, we run SpaCy to extract the entities from each of the sentences. For each sentence, we store the entity types and entities in a database record. SpaCy will have a technical limitation on the length of the documents it analyzes; therefore, we cut the very long text chunk into different chunks to respect the technical limitation. However, this comes with the price of chopping sentences at the cut-off point of the text chunk. Considering that we are handling hundreds of pages, we will take the short cut. Of course, the best way to cut this is to cut it approximately around the chunk, while respecting the punctuation in order to preserve the complete sentences.

The following code snippet depicts how to extract various entities:

```
''' *************************************
#2. NLP


'''
#Named Entity Extraction
print('ner')
#see if we need to convert everything to lower case words - we keep the
original format for this case
lower=False
common_words, sentences, words_list,verbs_list =
entitiesExtraction.NER_topics(text,lower)
entities_in_sentences = entitiesExtraction.org_extraction(text)
...
#create this list to export the list of ent and cleanse them
...
print('looping sentences')
for sentence in entities_in_sentences:
    ents_dict[sentence_cnt] = {}
    for entity in sentence:
        ...
```

```
if ent_type in( 'ORG','PERSON','FAC','NORP','GPE','LOC','PRODUCT'):
    ...
#handle other type
...
```

> **Entity classification via the lexicon:** For our use case, we need to further classify the organizations as suppliers, customers, competitors, investors, governments, or sister companies/assets—for example, banks that are the credit investors of the company will first be classified as **Banks** before they are inferred as the Credit Investors/Bankers for the company in its annual report. So some of the relationships require us to check against a database of organizations to classify them further. Acquiring such knowledge requires us to download the relevant databases—in our case, we use Wikipedia to download the list of banks. Only when we check against the list of names of banks will we be able to classify the organization as banks or not. We did not perform this step in our example, as we do not have the lexicon set that is normally available to banks.

Using NetworkX to store the network structure

After processing the data, the entities will be stored in SQL databases and further analyzed by NetworkX—a Python package that handles network data. Edge and Node are the building blocks of any graph; however, there are a lot more indicators to measure and describe the graph, as well as the position of the node and edge within the graph. What matters for our work now is to see whether the nodes are connected to the company in focus, and the type of connection they have.

At the end of NetworkX, the graph data is still pretty abstract. We need better interactive software to query and handle the data. Therefore, we will output the data as a CSV for Neo4j to further handle, as it provides a user interface to interact with the data.

It is, however, still far from being used—a lot of time is required to cleanse the dataset and define the types of relationship involved. Neo4j is a full-blown graph database that could satisfy the complex relationship structures.

A relationship must be established between the entities mentioned in the company's annual report and the entities stored in the database. In our example, we did not do any filtering of entities as the NLP model in the previous step has a lift of 85%, and so it does not have perfect performance when it comes to spotting the entities. We extract only the people and organizations as entities. For the type of relationship (edge), we do not differentiate between the different edge types.

After defining the network structure, we prepare a list that stores the nodes and edges and generates a graph via `matplotlib`, which itself is not sufficient for manipulation or visualization. Therefore, we output the data from NetworkX to CSV files—one storing the nodes and the other one storing the edges.

The following is the code snippet for generating a network of entities:

```
'''***************************************
#1. Import relevant libraries and variables

'''
#generate network
import sqlite3
import pandas as pd
import networkx as nx
import matplotlib.pyplot as plt

#db file
db_path = 'parsed_network.db'
db_name = 'network_db'

#sql db
conn = sqlite3.connect(db_path)
c = conn.cursor()

...

network_dict={}
edge_list=[]
curr_source =''
curr_entity = ''
org_list = []
person_list = []

'''***************************************
#2. generate the network with all entities connected to Duke Energy - whose
annual report is parsed

'''
target_name = 'Duke Energy'
#loop through the database to generate the network format data
for index, row in df_org.iterrows():
    ...

#Generate the output in networkX
print('networkx')
```

```
#output the network
G = nx.from_edgelist(edge_list)
pos = nx.spring_layout(G)
nx.draw(G, with_labels=False, nodecolor='r',pos=pos, edge_color='b')
plt.savefig('network.png')
```

Using Neo4j for graph visualization and querying

We will install Neo4j and import the CSV files to construct the data network in Neo4j—the industry-grade graph database. Unfortunately, Neo4j itself requires another set of programming languages to manipulate its data, called **Cypher**. This allows us to extract and search the data we need.

We generate the files required for Neo4j. The following code snippet initializes Neo4j:

```
#Generate output for Neo4j
print('prep data for Neo4j')
f_org_node=open('node.csv','w+')
f_org_node.write('nodename\n')

f_person_node=open('node_person.csv','w+')
f_person_node.write('nodename\n')

f_vertex=open('edge.csv','w+')
f_vertex.write('nodename1,nodename2,weight\n')
...
```

In the terminal, we copy the output files to the home directory of Neo4j. The following are the commands to be executed from the terminal:

```
sudo cp '[path]/edge.csv' /var/lib/Neo4j/import/edge.csv
sudo cp '[path]/node.csv' /var/lib/Neo4j/import/node.csv

sudo service Neo4j restart
```

At Neo4j, we log in via the browser. The following is the URL to enter into the browser:

```
http://localhost:7474/browser/
```

The following is the sample code snippet for Neo4j Cypher:

```
MATCH (n) DETACH DELETE n;

USING PERIODIC COMMIT
LOAD CSV WITH HEADERS FROM "file:///node.csv" AS row
CREATE (:ENTITY {node: row.nodename});
```

```
CREATE INDEX ON :ENTITY(node);


USING PERIODIC COMMIT
LOAD CSV WITH HEADERS FROM "file:///edge.csv" AS row
MATCH (vertex1:ENTITY {node: row.nodename1})
MATCH (vertex2:ENTITY {node: row.nodename2})
MERGE (vertex1)-[:LINK]->(vertex2);

MATCH (n:ENTITY)-[:LINK]->(ENTITY) RETURN n;
```

The following screenshot is the resulting output:

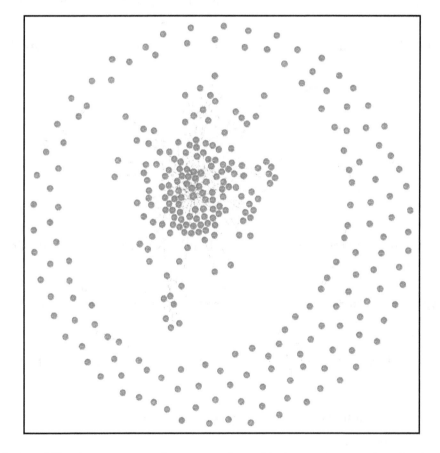

Congratulations! You have managed to extract lots of important names/parties from the annual report that you need to focus your research on for further analysis.

Summary

In this chapter, we learned about the behavior of the sell side of a market. We learned about what sentiment analysis is and how to use it. We also looked at an example to sense market needs using sentiment analysis. We learned about network analysis using Neo4j, which is a NoSQL database technique. We learned about text mining using the PDF miner tool.

In the next chapter, we will learn how to use bank APIs to build personal wealth advisers. Consumer banking will be a focus of the chapter. We will learn how to access the Open Bank Project to retrieve financial health data. We will also learn about document layout analysis in the chapter. Let's jump into it without any further ado.

8
Building Personal Wealth Advisers with Bank APIs

In the previous chapter, we analyzed the behavior of a sell-side of the exchange. We also learned about sentiment analysis and gained in-depth knowledge of the subject by learning how to analyze market needs using sentiment analysis. We then learned a bit about Neo4j, which is a NoSQL database technique. We then used Neo4j to build and store a network of entities involved in security trading.

In this chapter, we will focus on consumer banking and understand the needs of managing customer's digital data. Then, we will learn how to access the Open Bank Project, an open source platform for open banking. After that, we'll look at an example of wrapping AI models around bank APIs. Finally, we will learn about document layout analysis.

We will cover the following topics in this chapter:

- Managing customer's digital data
- The Open Bank Project
- Performing document layout analysis
- Cash flow projection using the Open Bank API
- Using invoice entity recognition to track daily expenses

Let's get started!

Managing customer's digital data

In this era of digitization, there is no reason that money cannot be 100% transparent or that money transfers can't happen in real time, 24/7. Consumers have the right to their data as it represents their identity. Whether it is possible to or not, we should be consolidating our own data – realistically, this should be happening today and in the coming few years. It is best to consolidate our banking data in one place; for example, our frequent flyer mileage. The key point is that there shall be two tiers of data architecture – one for consolidation (including storage) and another for running the artificial intelligence services that will be used to analyze the data through the use of a smart device, also known as **mobile applications**. It can be painful to design an AI algorithm without understanding what is going on at the data consolidation layer.

Here, our data source could be identity data, bio/psychometric data, financial data, events that could impact any of this static data, and social data, which represents our relationship with others (including humans, objects, living organisms, and so on). This is, in fact, very similar to a **business-to-business (B2B)** setting, where any corporation could be represented by its legal identity, shareholders/ownership structures, financial health, events, as well as its commercial relationship, as outlined in Chapter 7, *Sensing Market Sentiment for Algorithmic Marketing at Sell-Side*. This also means that what we are learning in this chapter can help with your understanding of the previous chapters in this book.

However, for all individuals, including your, our financial needs are quite basic—they include payment, credit, and wealth. These spell out the core activities of financial services. Insurance is included as part of wealth as it aims to protect our wealth against undesirable events and risks—it's like the derivatives that hedge risked on procurement costs in Chapter 2, *Time Series Analysis*.

However, I am also of the opinion that the data that's derived from consumers is also owned by the bank processing the transaction. It's like parenthood—all decisions regarding data (the parent's children) are agreed upon between the data owner (the consumer) and the data producer (the bank). What is lacking today is the technology to quickly attribute the data and economic benefits of the use of this data to certain economic activities, such as marketing. If one organization (for example, a supermarket) is paying social media (for example, Google, Facebook, and Twitter) for consumer's data for marketing purposes, the data owner will be credited with a portion of the economic benefits. Without advances in data technology, mere legal regulations will not be practical.

The Open Bank Project

The world's most advanced policy that allows consumers to consolidate their own data is called the **Open Banking Project**. It started in the UK in 2016, following the European's Directive PSD2 – the revised Payment Services Directive (`https://www.ecb.europa.eu/paym/intro/mip-online/2018/html/1803_revisedpsd.en.html`). This changed the competitive landscape of banks by lowering the entry barrier in terms of making use of banks' information for financial advisory reasons. This makes robo-advisors a feasible business as the financial data that banks contain is no longer segregated.

The challenge with this project is that the existing incumbent dominant banks have little incentive to open up their data. On the consumer side, the slowness in data consolidation impacts the economic values of this inter-connected network of financial data on banking services. This obeys Metcalfe's Law, which states that the value of a network is equivalent to the square number of connected users (in our case, banks). The following table analyzes the situation using Game Theory to anticipate the outcome for both banks and consumers—assuming that consumers have only two banks in the market with four possible outcomes:

Cell value = benefits of bank A/bank B/Consumer	Bank B: Open Bank API	Bank B: Not Open Bank API
Bank A: Open Bank API	0.5\0.5\2	0.5\1\1
Bank A: Not Open Bank API	1\0.5\1	1\1\1

For the status quo (that is, without any Open Bank API), let's assume that both banks A and B will enjoy 1 unit of benefits while the consumers will also have 1 unit of benefits.

For any bank to develop an Open Bank API, they will need to consume 0.5 of its resources. Therefore, we will have two cells showing either bank A or B developing the Open Bank API while the other does not. The one developing Open Bank API will have fewer benefits since 0.5 of the original 1 unit will need to be spent as resources to maintain the API. In these two cases, consumers cannot enjoy any additional benefits as the data is not consolidated.

Only in the case where all banks are adopting the Open Bank API will the consumers see incremental benefits (let's assume there's one more unit so that there's two in total, just to be arbitrary), while both banks have fewer benefits. This, of course, could be wrong as the market as a whole shall be more competitive, which is what is happening in the UK with regard to virtual banking—a new sub-segment has been created because of this initiative! So, at the end of the day, all banks could have improved benefits.

Having said that, the reality for most incumbent banks is that they have to maintain two sets of banking services—one completely virtual while the other set of banking channels remains brick and mortar and not scalable. Perhaps the way forward is to build another banking channel outside of its existing one and transfer the clients there.

Since a truly ideal state hasn't been achieved yet, for the moment, to construct a Digital You, there needs to be data from the **Open Bank Project** (**OBP**) from the UK on financial transactions (`https://uk.openbankproject.com/`), identity verification via Digidentity from the EU (`https://www.digidentity.eu/en/home/`), health records stored with IHiS from Singapore (`https://www.ihis.com.sg/`), events and social data from Facebook, Twitter, Instagram, and LinkedIn, life events from insurance companies, and so on. In short, we still need to work on each respective system rollout before we unite all these data sources.

Smart devices – using APIs with Flask and MongoDB as storage

Your smart device is a personalized private banker: the software will interact with markets and yourself. Within the smart device, the core modules are the **Holding** and **User Interaction** modules. The **Holding** module will safeguard the investment of the user/customer, while the user's interactions and the user themselves are greeted and connected by the **User Interaction** module.

The **Holding** module handles the quantitative aspect of investments—this is exactly what we covered in the previous two chapters, but at a personal level—by managing the portfolio and capturing various market data. However, the difference is that we need to understand the user/customer better through behavioral data that's been captured in the **User Interaction** module. The **Holding** module is the cognitive brain of the smart device.

The **User Interaction** module provides, of course, the interaction aspect of a smart device—it understands the user's preferences on investment and interactions. These investment preferences are captured in the **Investment Policy Statement** (**IPS**). These interactions are then handled by the **Behavior Analyzer**, which analyzes the preferred time, channels, and messages to communicate, as well as the financial behaviors of the user regarding their actual personality and risk appetite, both of which are derived from the data that's obtained from the **Data Feeds** of external sources or user-generated data from using the device. Last but not least, the **communication channels** (**Comm Channels**) interact with the user either by voice, text, or perhaps physically via a physical robot.

This sums up nicely what we mentioned in Chapter 1, *The Importance of AI in Banking*, as the definition of AI—a machine that thinks and acts like a human, either rationally or emotionally, or both. The **Holding** module is the rational brain of a human and acts accordingly in the market, while its emotions are handled by the **User Interaction** module – sympathized by the **Behavior Analyzer** and how they interact via the **Comm Channels**. The following diagram shows the market and user interaction through banking functions:

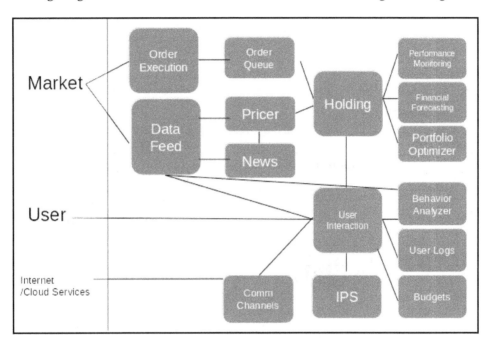

Since we've already talked about the **Holding** module in the previous two chapters, which focused on the investment process, here, we'll focus more on the **User Interaction** module. Specifically, we will dig deeper into **IPS**, which records the investment needs of the user.

Understanding IPS

As we mentioned in Chapter 6, *Automated Portfolio Management Using Treynor-Black Model and ResNet*, we will start looking at the individual's investment policy statement here. To do this, we need to collect data to build up the IPS for an individual customer.

Here is what it takes to build an IPS for a family:

- **Return and risk objectives**:

Objective	Comment
Return objectives	To be inputted by the investors and via the behavioral analyzer—personality profiling
Ability to take risk	To be inputted by the investors and via the behavioral analyzer—personality profiling
Willingness to take risk	To be inputted by the investors and via the behavioral analyzer—personality profiling

- **Constraints**:

Constraint	Comment
Liquidity	Liquidity of assets can be determined by the prices within the smart device.
Time horizon	Plan for your children's future – their studies (where and which school, how much, and so on), housing plans, jobs, retirement, and so on.
Taxes (both US citizens)	Citizenship via Digidentity.
Legal & regulatory environment	This could be implicated via commercial transactions, citizenship, employment, and residential constraints. You may also need to consider the legal entity that will manage your wealth, such as a family trust.
Unique circumstances	Interests and special circumstances aren't made known, including social media or medical profiles that stand out from a *standard* user's – this needs to be compared across users anonymously to provide real, unique circumstances.

Behavioral Analyzer – expenditure analyzers

Similar to `Chapter 2`, *Time Series Analysis*, we are going to forecast the day-to-day cash flow in the market. Since the income for most cases (and even most of the population who are working on salary) are fixed on a monthly basis, the only moving parts are the expenditures. Within these expenditures, there could be regular spending costs for things such as groceries, as well as irregular spending costs for things such as buying white goods or even a car. For a machine to track and project regular spending habits, as well as infrequent spending, the practical approach is to record these habits efficiently when they occur.

Exposing AI services as APIs

While the portfolio optimization model we built in `Chapter 6`, *Automated Portfolio Management Using Treynor-Black Model and ResNet*, was great, the key technology that will be addressed in this chapter will demonstrate how AI models are wrapped and provided to users via API. With regard to technical modeling skills, we are not going to add any new techniques to our repertoire in this chapter.

Performing document layout analysis

In ML, there is a discipline called **document layout analysis**. It is indeed about studying how humans understand documents. It includes computer vision, natural language processing, and knowledge graphs. The end game is to deliver an ontology that can allow any document to be navigated, similar to how word processors can, but in an automated manner. In a word processor, we have to define certain words that are found in headers, as well as within different levels of the hierarchy – for example, heading level 1, heading level 2, body text, paragraph, and so on. What's not defined manually by humans is sentences, vocabulary, words, characters, pixels, and so on. However, when we handle the images taken by a camera or scanner, the lowest level of data is a pixel.

Steps for document layout analysis

In this section, we will learn how to perform document layout analysis. The steps are as follows:

1. **Forming characters from pixels**: The technique, which is used to convert pixels into characters, is known as **Optical Character Recognition** (**OCR**). It is a well-known problem that can be solved by many examples of deep learning, including the MNIST dataset. Alternatively, we could use Tesseract-OCR to perform OCR.

2. **Image rotation**: When the image is not located at the correct vertical orientation, it may create challenges for people to read the characters. Of course, new research in this area is occurring that seems to be able to skip this step.

3. **Forming words from characters**: Practically, we cannot wait minutes upon minutes for this to happen; with human performance, we can get this right. How do we know that a character shall be banded together with other characters to form one word? We know this from spatial clues. Yet the distance between characters is not fixed, so how can we teach a machine to understand this spatial distance? This is perhaps the challenge most people suffering from dyslexia face. Machines also suffer from dyslexia by default.

4. **Building meaning from words**: This requires us to know the topic of the paper and the spelling of the words, which helps us to check our various dictionaries to understand what the document is about. *Learning* (in terms of deep learning in this book) could mean just a topic related to education, and the reason we know that it because you understand that this book is a machine learning book by Packt – a publisher name that you learned about in the past. Otherwise, by merely reading the word Packt, we may guess that it is related to a packaging company (that is, PACK-t)? In addition, we also draw clues from the label words—*step 3* itself looks like label words that introduce the actual content on the right-hand side of it.

Classifying words as various generic types of entities helps – for example, dates, serial numbers, dollar amount, time, and so on. These are the generic entities we typically see in open source spaces such as spaCy, which we used in `Chapter 7`, *Sensing Market Sentiment for Algorithmic Marketing at Sell Side*.

With regard to spatial clues in the form of words, we may understand the importance of larger words while paying less attention to smaller words. The location of the words on the page matter too. For example, to read English, we normally read from top to bottom, left to right, while in some other languages, we need to read from right to left, top to bottom, such as ancient Chinese.

Using Gensim for topic modeling

In our example of topic modeling, we will focus on *step 4* to limit our scope of work. We will do this while we take the prework from *steps 1* to *3* for granted and skip *steps 5* and *6*. The dataset image we will be using has already been cleaned, rotated, and OCRed – this included binding characters to form words. What we have at hand is a dataset with each record represented by a text block, which could include multiple words. Gensim is concerned with tracking nouns in text.

Vector dimensions of Word2vec

Word2Vec defines words by their different features – the feature value of each word is defined by the distance between the words that appear in the same sentence. It is meant to quantify the similarity between concepts and topics. In our example of Word2vec, we will use a pre-trained model to convert text into words. However, for each text block, there may be several values involved. In such a case, a series of these vectors would be compressed into a value, using a value called an **Eigenvalue**. We will use this simple approach to perform dimension reduction, which we do when we want to reduce the number of features (dimensions) of a variable. The most common approach to dimension reduction is called **Principal Component Analysis** (**PCA**). It is mostly applied to scalars, not vectors of variables. Imagine that each word is represented by a vector. Here, one text block with two words will be represented by a matrix composed of two vectors. Therefore, the PCA may not be an ideal solution for this kind of dimension reduction task.

While interpreting the vectors that represent the topic of the word, it is important to analyze the dimensions involved, as each dimension represents one semantic/meaning group. In our example of Word2vec, we'll skip this step to avoid putting too many dimensions into the meaningful extraction process. This means we'll have smaller feature spaces for illustration purposes.

Cash flow projection using the Open Bank API

In the future, we will need robo-advisors to be able to understand our needs. The most basic step is to be able to pull our financial data from across banks. Here, we will assume that we are customers of consumer banking services from the US who are staying in the UK. We are looking for wealth planning for a family of four—a married couple and two kids. What we want is a robo-advisor to perform all our financial activities for us.

We will retrieve all the necessary transaction data from the **Open Bank Project (OBP)** API to forecast our expenditure forecasting via Open Bank API. The data that we will be using will be simulated data that follows the format specified in the OBP. We are not going to dive deep into any of the software technologies while focusing on building the wealth planning engine. The family description we'll be using has been obtained from the Federal Reserve (`https://www.federalreserve.gov/econresdata/2016-economic-well-being-of-us-households-in-2015-Income-and-Savings.htm`) regarding American household financials.

The following table shows the typical values of households in the US, which helps us understand the general demand for consumer banking:

Income/Expense	Value (In US $)	Data Source (OBS)
Income	**102.7**	
Salaries from working people	102.7	Largest auto-payment every month, with fixed salaries on a monthly basis.
Living expenses	**67.3**	
Annual expenses	57.3	Retrieve all transactions from credit cards, savings, and current accounts.
Debt repayment	10.0	Transactions related to debt account.
Net worth	**97**	
Assets	**189.9**	
Financial assets	23.5	The outstanding balance of Securities account. No visibility of the 401 plan.
Non-financial assets	158.9	Housing valuation provided by Zillow.
Liabilities	**92.6**	
Mortgage	59.5	The outstanding balance of the debt account.
Auto loans and educational debts	32.8	Auto loan: Outstanding balance of debt account; student loan (federal), with the counterpart being Federal Student loan's; Student loan (private): Outstanding balance of debt account.

For more details about Zillow, please refer to this link: `https://www.zillow.com/howto/api/APIOverview.htm`.

Steps involved

To use the Open Bank API, we will need to do the following:

1. Register to use the Open Bank API.
2. Download the necessary data.
3. Create a database to store this data.
4. Set up an API for forecasting.

Let's get started!

Registering to use Open Bank API

There are several ways we can access the Open Banking Project—we will work on one such where we registered at `https://demo.openbankproject.com/`.

Creating and downloading demo data

The code for this section can be downloaded from GitHub (`https://github.com/OpenBankProject/Hello-OBP-DirectLogin-Python`). Based on the `hello_obp.py` file from this repository, we have modified the program so that it downloads the required data. Use the following code snippet to download the demo data:

```
# -*- coding: utf-8 -*-

from __future__ import print_function     # (at top of module)
import sys
import time
import requests


# Note: in order to use this example, you need to have at least one account
# that you can send money from (i.e. be the owner).
# All properties are now kept in one central place

from props.default import *


# You probably don't need to change those
...

#add the following lines to hello-obp.py before running it
#add lines to download the file
```

```
print("")
print(" --- export json")
import json
f_json = open('transactions.json','w+')
json.dump(transactions,f_json,sort_keys=True, indent=4)
```

Creating a NoSQL database to store the data locally

I prefer MongoDB for this due to its ability to import JSON files in a hierarchical manner, without us needing to define the structure in advance. Even though we will need to store the NoSQL file in SQL database format (as we did in the previous chapter) whenever we need to run predictions with the ML model, it is still useful for us to cache the downloaded data physically before we run the prediction.

So, you may be wondering why we need to store it in a NoSQL database for our purposes – can't we just save it as we did in the previous chapter, when we handled tweet data? No – we want to use a database because for quicker retrieval, given that we will be storing hundreds of thousands of JSON files with an infinite number of days versus batch downloads. This also depends on how frequently we want to download the data; if we wish to update our databases every day, we may not need to store the JSON data in a NoSQL database as we wouldn't have very many files to deal with. However, if we are querying the data or continuously adding new features to the training dataset, we might be better off storing the raw data on our side.

The following code is used to establish our connectivity with the MongoDB server:

```
from pymongo import MongoClient
import json
import pprint

#client = MongoClient()
client = MongoClient('mongodb://localhost:27017/')
db_name = 'AIFinance8A'
collection_name = 'transactions_obp'

f_json = open('transactions.json', 'r')
json_data = json.loads(f_json)

...

#to check if all documents are inserted
...
```

The following code is used to create the database:

```
#define libraries and variables
import sqlite3
from pymongo import MongoClient
import json
from flatten_dict import flatten

client = MongoClient('mongodb://localhost:27017/')
db_name = 'AIFinance8A'
collection_name = 'transactions_obp'

db = client[db_name]
collection = db[collection_name]
posts = db.posts


...


#flatten the dictionary
...


#create the database schema
#db file
db_path = 'parsed_obp.db'
db_name = 'obp_db'

#sql db
...
sqlstr = 'drop table '+db_name
...
print('create')
...
#loop through the dict and insert them into the db
...

for cnt in dict_cnt:
    ...
    for fld in tuple_fields_list:
        ...
    ...
    sqlstr = 'insert into '+ db_name+ '(' + str(fld_list_str)+') VALUES \
                                    ('+question_len[1:]+')'
    ...
```

Setting up the API for forecasting

To perform forecasting for payments, we need to know what kind of forecasting model we want to build. Do we want a time series model or the ML model? Of course, we want to have a model that provides more information.

In our example, we have not prepared any model for this as the method we'll be using will be similar to the model we used in Chapter 2, *Time Series Analysis*. The main point to illustrate here is how to set up the API server and how to use another program to consume the API. Please make sure these two programs are run simultaneously.

The server will be set up to listen to requests so that it can run predictions. We will simply load the model without running any predictions. The following code snippet is used to connect us to the Open Bank API server:

```
#Libraries
from flask import Flask, request, jsonify
from sklearn.externals import joblib
import traceback
import pandas as pd
import numpy as np

# Your API definition
app = Flask(__name__)

@app.route('/predict', methods=['POST'])
def predict():
    ...

#Run the server
if __name__ == '__main__':
    ...
```

The following code snippet is used to create requests from the client application:

```
import requests

host = 'http://127.0.0.1:12345/'

r = requests.post(host+'predict', json={"key": "value"})
print(r)
```

Congratulations! You have built a robot that can read data from banks and have built it so that it can run AI models on this data.

For a household, it becomes critical to limit expenses to increase their cash flow. In the next section, we will look at how to track daily expenses using the invoice entity recognition technique.

Using invoice entity recognition to track daily expenses

While we are always dreaming for the end game of digitization through AI in finance, the reality is that there is data that's trapped. And very often, these expenses come in the form of paper, not API feeds. Dealing with paper would be inevitable if we were to transform ourselves into a fully digital world where all our information is stored in JSON files or SQL databases. We cannot avoid handling existing paper-based information. Using an example of a paper-based document dataset, we are going to demonstrate how to build up the engine for the invoice entity extraction model.

In this example, we will assume you are developing your own engine to scan and transform the invoice into a structured data format. However, due to a lack of data, you will need to parse the Patent images dataset, which is available at `http://machinelearning.inginf.units.it/data-and-tools/ghega-dataset`. Within the dataset, there are images, text blocks, and the target results that we want to extract from. This is known as **entity extraction**. The challenge here is that these invoices are not in a standardized format. Different merchants issue invoices in different sizes and formats, yet we are still able to understand the visual clues (font size, lines, positions, and so on) and the languages of the words and the words surrounding it (called **labels**).

Steps involved

We have to follow six steps to track daily expenses using invoice entity recognition. These steps are as follows:

1. Import the relevant libraries and define the variables. In this example, we're introducing topic modeling, including **Word to Vector** (`Word2vec`), using `gensim`, and regular expressions using `re`, a built-in module. The following code snippet is used to import the required libraries:

```
import os
import pandas as pd
from numpy import genfromtxt
import numpy as np
```

```
from gensim.models import Word2Vec
from gensim.models.keyedvectors import WordEmbeddingsKeyedVectors
import gensim.downloader as api
from gensim.parsing.preprocessing import remove_stopwords
from gensim.parsing.preprocessing import preprocess_string,
strip_tags,
remove_stopwords,strip_numeric,strip_multiple_whitespaces
from scipy import linalg as LA
import pickle
import re
from sklearn.model_selection import train_test_split
from sklearn.neural_network import MLPClassifier
from sklearn.preprocessing import StandardScaler
from sklearn.metrics import classification_report,roc_curve,
auc,confusion_matrix,f1_score

#please run this in terminal: sudo apt-get install libopenblas-dev
model_word2vec = api.load("text8") # load pre-trained words vectors
```

2. Define the functions that will need to be used later. There will be two groups of functions—one, 2A, is used to train and test the neural network, while the other, 2B, aims at converting the text into numeric values. The following code snippet defines the functions that will be used for invoice entity recognition:

```
#2. Define functions relevant for works
##2A Neural Network
##2A_i. Grid search that simulate the performance of different
neural network design
def grid_search(X_train,X_test,
Y_train,Y_test,num_training_sample):
...
##2A_ii train network
def train_NN(X,Y,target_names):
...
#2B: prepare the text data series into numeric data series
#2B.i: cleanse text by removing multiple whitespaces and converting
to lower cases
def cleanse_text(sentence,re_sub):
...
#2B.ii: convert text to numeric numbers
def text_series_to_np(txt_series,model,re_sub):
...
```

3. Prepare the dataset. In this example, we will try to use numpy to store the features as they're quite big. We will also use pandas for each file as it is far easier to manipulate and select columns using a DataFrame, given that the size of each image isn't too large. The following code snippet is used to prepare the dataset:

```
#3. Loop through the files to prepare the dataset for training and
testing
#loop through folders (represent different sources)
for folder in list_of_dir:
    files = os.path.join(path,folder)
    #loop through folders (represent different filing of the same
    source)
    for file in os.listdir(files):
        if file.endswith(truth_file_ext):
        #define the file names to be read
        ...

        #merge ground truth (aka target variables) with the blocks
        ...

        #convert the text itself into vectors and lastly a single
        value using Eigenvalue
        text_df = f_df['text']
        text_np = text_series_to_np(text_df,model_word2vec,re_sub)

        label_df = f_df['text_label']
        label_np = text_series_to_np(label_df, model_word2vec, \
                                     re_sub)
        ...
Y_pd = pd.get_dummies(targets_df)
Y_np = Y_pd.values
```

4. Execute the model. Here, we execute the model we prepared using the functions we defined in previous steps. The following code snippet is used to execute the model:

```
#4. Execute the training and test the outcome
NN_clf, f1_clf = train_NN(full_X_np,Y_np,dummy_header)
...
```

Congratulations! With that, you have built a model that can extract information from scanned images!

5. Draw the clues from the spatial and visual environment of the word. The preceding line clearly separates *steps 4* and *5*. Noticing how these lines are being projected also helps us group similar words together. For documents that require original copies, we may need to look at signatures and logos, as well as matching these against a true verified signature or stamp.

6. Construct a knowledge map of these documents. This is when we can build a thorough understanding of the knowledge embedded in the document. Here, we need to use the graph database to keep track of this knowledge (we covered this in the previous chapter).

This concludes our example of tracking daily expenses, as well as this chapter.

Summary

In this chapter, we covered how to extract data and provide AI services using APIs. We understood how important it is to manage customer's digital data. We also understood the Open Bank Project and document layout analysis. We learned about this through two examples—one was about projecting cash flows, while the other was about tracking daily expenses.

The next chapter will also focus on consumer banking. We will learn how to create proxy data for information that's missing in the customer's profile. We also will take a look at an example chatbot that we can use to serve and interact with customers. We will use graph and NLP techniques to create this chatbot.

Mass Customization of Client Lifetime Wealth

9

In the previous chapter, we learned how to manage the digital data of customers. We also covered the Open Bank Project and the Open Bank API. In addition, we learned about document layout analysis and looked at an example of projecting the cash flow for a typical household. Then, we looked at another example of how to track daily expenses using invoice entity recognition.

In this chapter, we will learn how to combine data from a survey for personal data analysis. We will learn techniques such as Neo4j, which is a graph database. We will build a chatbot to serve customers 24/7. We will also learn how to predict customer responses using NLP and Neo4j with the help of an example. After this, we will learn how to use cypher languages to manipulate data from the Neo4j database.

The following topics will be covered in this chapter:

- Financial concepts of wealth instruments
- Ensemble learning
- Predicting customer responses
- Building a chatbot to serve customers 24/7
- Knowledge management using NLP and graphs

Financial concepts of wealth instruments

In this section, we will be answering a few questions asked by a consumer bank's marketers. Then, we will look at another important model development technique—ensemble learning—which will be useful in combining predictions from different models.

Sources of wealth: asset, income, and gifted

One of the most common tasks in retail banking customer analytics is to retrieve additional data that helps us to explain the customers' investment behavior and patterns. No doubt we will know the response of the customers, but the work of a model is to find out why they respond as they do. Surprisingly, there is a lot of aggregated information concerning the behaviors of individuals, such as census data. We can also find data from social media, where users use social media for authentication. The relevant social media information can then be chained together with individual-level transactional data that we observed internally in the organization. To explain individual banking behaviors, the most relevant supplementary data that we want is the information regarding their wealth.

Customer life cycle

A typical life cycle involves three major phases—acquisition, cross-selling/upselling, and retention. The following diagram illustrates these three phases:

Acquisition is when we start a commercial relationship with customers. Then, we move on to **cross-selling** and **upselling**. Cross-selling is about improving the number of products/services that are sold to the customer. Up-selling is about deepening the wallet share of the same product with the products/services. **Retention** is about keeping the relationship and is a defensive act by the bank to protect the relationship. Our first example (described in the following section) concerns cross-selling (if the customers do not have the product) and up-selling (if the customers own the product).

Ensemble learning

Ensemble learning is the boosting technique that helps us in improving the accuracy of the prediction. We will also learn how to use the graph database for knowledge storage. Knowledge storage is the current challenge in knowledge representation that can be used to empower AI for professional-grade financial services.

Ensemble learning is an approach that is used to summarize several models in order to give a more stable prediction. It was a very common approach before deep neural networks became popular. For completeness, we do not want to ignore this modeling technique in this very short book. In particular, we have used random forest, which means that we build lots of decision trees as a forest and we apply logic to cut down trees that have lower performance. Another approach would be combining the weaker model to generate a strong result, which is called the **boosting method**. We won't cover it here, but readers are encouraged to dig deeper in the scikit-learn documentation (`https://scikit-learn.org/stable/`).

Knowledge retrieval via graph databases

To make a machine talk like a human in customer services, one of the key elements is the conversational component. When we engage in conversation, it is normal that human customers may not be able to provide the full amount of information required for processing. Humans can work with fuzziness. Humans can understand the context, and so can extrapolate meaning without the concepts being explicitly mentioned. Knowing that a machine can only solve definite problems while humans can work on fuzziness, it is the job of the machine to infer meaning from the knowledge map that it has for the customers. A graph database is used to serve this purpose.

Predict customer responses

So far, we have not talked about the day-to-day marketing activity of the bank. Now, we have finally come to look at how marketing prospects are determined. Even though each customer is unique, they are still handled by algorithms in the same way.

In this example, you will assume the role of a data scientist tasked with the marketing of a term deposit product. We are going to train the model to predict the marketing campaign for the term deposit. Data pertaining to the bank's internal data regarding customers and their previous responses to the campaign is obtained from the Center for Machine Learning and Intelligent Systems (`https://archive.ics.uci.edu/ml/datasets/bank+marketing`), the Bren School of Information and Computer Science, and the University of California, Irvine. Survey information about personal wealth is obtained from the US Census Bureau (`https://www.census.gov/data/tables/time-series/demo/income-poverty/historical-income-households.html`), which serves as an augmentation to the bank's internal data.

Solution

There are four steps to complete this example:

1. We introduce random forest, which is a type of machine learning algorithm that utilizes ensemble learning, allowing predictions to be made by multiple models. The resulting model is a combination of the results from the multiple models. The following is the code snippet to import the required libraries and define the variables:

```
#import libraries & define variables
import pandas as pd
import os
from sklearn.ensemble import RandomForestClassifier
from sklearn.datasets import make_classification
```

2. Census data provides information about the deposit and wealth of the age group placed in the bank. The following is the code snippet to handle census data:

```
cat_val = ''
cat_dict = {}
for index, row in df_xtics.iterrows():
    ...

df_bank['age_c'] = pd.cut(df_bank['age'],
[0,35,45,55,65,70,75,200])

#ID Conversions
df_bank['age_c_codes']=df_bank['age_c'].cat.codes.astype(str)
age_map={'0':'Less than 35 years'
,'1':'35 to 44 years'
,'2':'45 to 54 years'
,'3':'55 to 64 years'
,'4':'.65 to 69 years'
,'5':'.70 to 74 years'
,'6':'.75 and over'}
```

3. We want to illustrate the mapping of one column's data, using age to introduce wealth data. The following is the code snippet to combine census data with the bank's data:

```
#3. map back the survey data
df_bank['age_c1']=df_bank['age_c_codes'].map(age_map)
df_bank['age_c1_val']=df_bank['age_c1'].map(cat_dict['Age of
Householder'])

X_flds = ['balance','day', 'duration', 'pdays',
```

```
                    'previous', 'age_c1_val']
    X = df_bank[X_flds]
    y = df_bank['y']
```

4. The following is the code snippet to train the model:

```
X, y = make_classification(n_samples=1000, n_features=3,
                           n_informative=2, n_redundant=0,
                           random_state=0, shuffle=False)
clf = RandomForestClassifier(n_estimators=100, max_depth=2,
                             random_state=0)
clf.fit(X, y)
print(clf.feature_importances_)
```

Congratulations! You have merged an external dataset with the internal dataset to augment our understanding of the customers.

Building a chatbot to service customers 24/7

When we interact with a robot, we expect it to understand and speak to us. The beauty of having a robot work for us is that it could serve us 24 hours a day throughout the week. Realistically, chatbots nowadays interact poorly with customers, and so we should try to break down the components of these chatbots to raise the bar to a higher standard. For an application-type development, you could use Google Assistant, Amazon's Alexa, or IBM Watson. But for learning purposes, let's break down the components and focus on the key challenges:

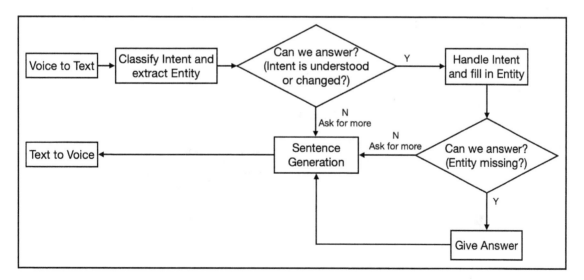

The chatbot performs two operations at a high level. One is to convert an input from voice to text, and another one is to translate an output from text to voice. Both of these operations involve extracting the entity and understanding the intent. In this example, the resulting text is an entity, whereas the meaning of the text is an intent. It represents a conversation between the service requester and the service provider. When faced with an incoming service request, the chatbot converts the voice instructions into text and adds context to the information received. Once the context building is done, the chatbot processes the information to generate the output in text format. The chatbot has to convert it into an audible voice output to be presented to the service requester. The whole scenario is explained in the preceding diagram.

Right now, let's focus on chat only, without worrying about voice recognition and utterance—that is, let's ignore voice to text and text to voice. In my opinion, since this task is machine- and memory-intensive, and the data is available in so many places, it is not for a start-up to work on this task; instead, we should leave it to a mainstream cloud provider with a strong infrastructure to deliver the service.

For text-only chat, the key focus should be on intent classification and entity extraction. While we have touched on entity extraction in the previous chapter, the input still needs to be classified before it is extracted. Intent classification works similarly to entity extraction, but treats the whole sentence as an entity for classification.

While it is very common to run a chatbot using ChatterBot or RasaNLU, we can break down the components to run from the bottom up.

Let's say that we are a simple bank that offers deposits and loans. We are building a simple chatbot that can serve existing customers only, and at the moment, we only have two customers, one called **abc** with a deposit account, and another called **bcd** with a loan account:

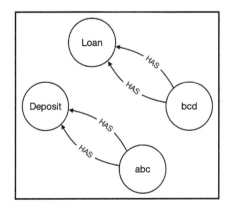

Abc's deposit has an outstanding balance of 100 units and a pricing of 1, and bcd has an outstanding loan of 100 units and a pricing of 2.

Knowledge management using NLP and graphs

Essentially, there are two ways for us to retrieve and update knowledge about our real world. One is to store the knowledge in vector space and read the file to our memory during runtime using programs such as Word2Vector and BERT. Another approach is to load the knowledge into a graph database, such as Neo4j, and retrieve and query the data. The strength and weakness of both approaches lies in speed and transparency. For high-speed subject classification, in-memory models fare better, but for tasks that require transparency, such as banking decisions, the updating of data requires full transparency and permanent record keeping. In these cases, we will use a graph database. However, like the example we briefly covered in `Chapter 7`, *Sensing Market Sentiment for Algorithmic Marketing at Sell Side*, NLP is required to extract information from the document before we can store the information in graph format.

Practical implementation

The following are the steps to complete this example:

1. Use the Cypher languages to import `csv` files into the database. We assume that the CSV file is dumped from the traditional SQL database. The following are the commands to be executed from the command line:

```
sudo cp dataset.csv /var/lib/Neo4j/import/edge.csv
sudo cp product.csv /var/lib/Neo4j/import/product.csv
sudo cp customer.csv /var/lib/Neo4j/import/customer.csv
```

2. Open the browser and navigate to `http://localhost:7474/browser/`. Then, create a `username` and set a `password`. This will be executed only once:

```
username: test, password: test
```

3. Delete all nodes:

```
MATCH (n) DETACH DELETE n;
```

4. Create customer data:

```
LOAD CSV WITH HEADERS FROM "file:///customer.csv" AS row
CREATE (c:Customer {customer_id: row.customer});
```

5. Create product data:

```
LOAD CSV WITH HEADERS FROM "file:///product.csv" AS row
CREATE (p:Product {product_name: row.product});
```

6. Load the CSV file:

```
LOAD CSV WITH HEADERS FROM "file:///edge.csv" AS line
WITH line
MATCH (c:Customer {customer_id:line.customer})
MATCH (p:Product {product_name:line.product})
MERGE (c)-[:HAS {TYPE:line.type, VALUE:toInteger(line.value)}]->(p)
RETURN count(*);
```

7. Match and return the data:

```
MATCH (c)-[cp]->(p) RETURN c,cp,p;
```

Cypher is a language in itself; what we do is essentially create the product and customers. Then, we load another file that connects customers to products.

8. We will connect to the Neo4j database that we just populated with data. The parameters follow the default setting. Please note the unique syntax of Cypher. In addition, the NLP model is loaded to be used for similarity analysis of the inputted instruction. The Cypher queries are stored in a dictionary. After the intent is read, the query string is retrieved. Then, we build the knowledge using the graph database:

```
#import libraries and define parameters
from Neo4j import GraphDatabase
import spacy

#define the parameters, host, query and keywords
uri = "bolt://localhost:7687"
driver = GraphDatabase.driver(uri, auth=("test", "test"))
session = driver.session()

check_q = ("MATCH (c:Customer)-[r:HAS]->(p:Product)"
  "WHERE c.customer_id = $customerid AND p.product_name = \
   $productname"
  "RETURN DISTINCT properties(r)")
...
```

```
intent_dict = {'check':check_q, 'login':check_c}

#list of key intent, product and attribute
product_list = ['deposit','loan']
attribute_list = ['pricing','balance']
intent_list = ['check']
print('loading nlp model')
nlp = spacy.load('en_core_web_md')
```

9. Users should be authenticated and identified properly using the SQL database. For ease of illustration, we will use `GraphDatabase`, but it is quite clear that using `GraphDatabase` for authentication is not right because we want to store a huge amount of data with usernames and passwords in a dedicated table whose access rights we can set to fewer individuals than the total number of people on the database. The following is the code snippet to authenticate the user:

```
if name == '' or reset:
    name = input('Hello, What is your name? ')
    print('Hi '+name)
    #check for login
    query_str = intent_dict['login']
    result = session.read_transaction(run_query, query_str, name, \
                             product, attribute, attribute_val)
```

Sentence intent and entity extraction utilizes spaCy on similarity analysis. Based on a pretrained word-to-vector model, the reserved words on intents and entities are compared with the inputted sentence to extract the relevant intent and entities. The model is overly simplified as readers are left with a lot of creative space to enhance the extraction works by using a better language model, such as BERT, on the assumption that we have made the relevant model to perform the relevant classification task.

The following is the code snippet to extract entities and add intent:

```
#Sentences Intent and Entities Extraction
input_sentence = input('What do you like to do? ')
if input_sentence == "reset":
    reset = True
entities = intent_entity_attribute_extraction(nlp, input_sentence, \
                        tokens_intent, tokens_products, tokens_attribute)
#actually can build another intent classifier here based on the scores and
words matched as features, as well as previous entities
intent = entities[0]
product = entities[1]
attribute = entities[2]
attribute_val = entities[3]
```

Cross-checking and further requesting missing information

The program will continuously ask for intents, products, and attributes until all three pieces of information are clear to the program. Underneath the classification of each of these parameters, we deploy Word2vec for simplified classification. In fact, we can run a best-in-class topic classification model, such as BERT, to understand the languages and topics.

The following is the code snippet to request missing information from the user:

```
while intent == '':
    input_sentence = input('What do you want to do?')
    entities = intent_entity_attribute_extraction(nlp, input_sentence, \
                    tokens_intent, tokens_products, tokens_attribute)
    intent = entities[0]

while product == '':
    input_sentence = input('What product do you want to check?')
    entities = intent_entity_attribute_extraction(nlp, input_sentence, \
                    tokens_intent, tokens_products, tokens_attribute)
    product = entities[1]

while attribute == '':
    input_sentence = input('What attribute of the ' + product + \
                    ' that you want to '+intent+'?')
    entities = intent_entity_attribute_extraction(nlp, input_sentence, \
                    tokens_intent, tokens_products, tokens_attribute)
    attribute = entities[2]
```

Extracting the answer

When all information is filled in, the Cypher query will be executed and the information will be presented to the user. The following is the code snippet to extract the answer:

```
#execute the query to extract the answer
query_str = intent_dict[intent]
results = session.read_transaction(run_query, query_str, name, \
                                    product,attribute,attribute_val)
if len(results) >0:
    for result in results:
        if result['TYPE'] == attribute:
            print(attribute + ' of ' + product + ' is '+ \
                str(result['VALUE']))
else:
    print('no record')
```

Sample script of interactions

The following snippet shows the users' output and input. It is meant to show that the NLU can indeed extract intent and entities using closely associated words, thanks to the spaCy dictionary that allows us to find similar words. The whole point of the example is to show that for decisions requiring complete information before they are made, the graph database allows us to manage the dialogue and follow up with the missing information before any instructions are executed to serve the user. This is a very important feature when it comes to making professional decisions where we need its rationale to be transparent to a high degree of accuracy, as far as the machine can understand the language. The following is a snippet of the sample conversation of the chatbot:

```
loading nlp model
Hello, What is your name? testing
Hi testing
Failed to find testing
Hello, What is your name? abc
Hi abc
What do you like to do? do sth
matching...

What do you want to do?check sth
matching...
check
What product do you want to check?some product
matching...

What product do you want to check?deposit
matching...
 deposit
What attribute of the deposit that you want to check?sth
matching...

What attribute of the deposit that you want to check?pricing
matching...
 pricing
pricing of deposit is 1
```

Congratulations! You have built a very simple chatbot that can show you the core functionality of chatbots.

The example we are using is a very good echo of what we start with in commercial banking in terms of using borrowers' and depositors' data using reinforcement learning. Back then, the data was stored in variables at runtime. Right now, we have demonstrated another possibility for storing the data in graph data. Indeed, compared to the example in Chapter 3, *Using Features and Reinforcement Learning to Automate Bank Financing,* the speed of reinforcement learning will be slower if we were to store data in a graph database rather than variables in a Python program. Therefore, we will use a graph database, but only for production and application levels when individual dialogues can tolerate some delay compared with a computation-intensive training phase.

Summary

In this chapter, we learned about NLP and graph databases and we learned about the financial concepts that are required to analyze customer data. We also learned about an artificial intelligence technique called ensemble learning. We looked at an example where we predicted customer responses using natural language processing. Lastly, we built a chatbot to serve requests from customers 24/7. These concepts are very powerful. NLP is capable of enabling programs to interpret languages that humans speak naturally. The graph database, on the other hand, is helpful in designing highly efficient algorithms.

In the next chapter, we will learn about practical considerations to bear in mind when you want to build a model to solve your day-to-day challenges. In addition, we also want to look at the practical IT considerations when equipping data scientists with languages to interact with IT developers who put the algorithm to use in real life.

10
Real-World Considerations

This chapter serves as the conclusion of the book. It wraps up the near-term banking world we will soon be living in. We will also add some useful tips on the considerations required to incorporate these AI engines in day-to-day production environments. This part corresponds to the business understanding step of the CRISP-DM, the approach for implementing any data mining project that we introduced in Chapter 1, *The Importance of AI in Banking*.

In this chapter, we will first summarize the techniques and knowledge that you learned throughout chapters 2 to 9, and then we will cover the forward-looking topics that will be an extension of our journey in banking. These are the topics and knowledge that will be covered:

- Summary of techniques covered
- Impact on banking professionals, regulators, and governments
- How to come up with features and acquire the domain knowledge
- IT production considerations in connection with AI deployment
- Where to look for more use cases
- Which areas require more practical research?

Summary of techniques covered

Following along the business segments of banking, we have covered quite a lot of data and AI techniques. We have also gone through the models with minimal use of complex formula or jargons.

AI modeling techniques

We have covered statistical models, optimization, and machine learning models. Within machine learning models, we covered unsupervised, supervised, and reinforcement learning. In terms of the type of data the supervised learning models run on, we covered structured data, images, and languages (NLP). With regard to data processing, we have also covered a number of sampling and testing approaches that help us. We will now recap the AI modeling techniques covered in the book so far:

- Starting with supervised learning, this is a technique of labeling the input data prior to processing. The model is built to learn from the labels so that labeling will be done automatically with the next set of input data. Unsupervised learning, on the other hand, does not label the input data. It does not have labeled or trained data. Processing is effected by identifying objects based on patterns and repetitions.

- Reinforcement learning is based on reaching the next immediate goal and assessing the distance from the final goal. This technique requires immediate feedback or input from the user to reach the final goal.

- An artificial neural network is a concept that mimics the neural network in the human brain. The neurons in the human brain are represented by nodes in the artificial neural network.

- Deep learning is one of the areas in machine learning and artificial neural networks. Deep learning algorithms use multiple layers to extract higher-level information from the raw input data.

- CRISP-DM is a standard for data mining. It stands for *cross-industry standard for data mining*. It provides a structured approach to planning data mining and data analysis projects.

- Time series analysis is a prediction technique that relies on historical data captured at a specific interval in time. In time series analysis, we decide on an observation parameter and capture the values of the parameter at a specific time interval. An example of this could be monthly expenses captured by a branch of a bank.

- NLP is concerned with the conversation between human languages and machine languages. A speech-to-text engine capable of understanding and interpreting human voice and perform commands can be an example of NLP.

- Finally, ensemble learning uses multiple machine learning algorithms to obtain better predictions in comparison to predictions obtained by using single machine learning algorithms.

Impact on banking professionals, regulators, and government

We have embarked on a long journey through commercial banking (Chapter 2, *Time Series Analysis* and Chapter 3, *Using Features and Reinforcement Learning to Automate Bank Financing*), investment banking (Chapter 4, *Mechanizing Capital Market Decisions* and Chapter 5, *Predicting the Future of Investment Bankers*), security sales and trading (Chapter 6, *Automated Portfolio Management Using Treynor-Black Model and ResNet* and Chapter 7, *Sensing Market Sentiment for Algorithmic Marketing at Sell Side*), and consumer banking (Chapter 8, *Building Personal Wealth Advisers with Bank APIs* and Chapter 9, *Mass Customization of Client Lifetime Wealth*) within the banking industry. This section accompanies a sample corporate client—Duke Energy—on its journey from commercial banking through to investment banking. In investment banking, we begin by introducing the investment communities who are on the buying side of the securities issued by corporate, before shifting to the investment side completely in Chapter 6, *Automated Portfolio Management Using Treynor-Black Model and ResNet* and Chapter 7, *Sensing Market Sentiment for Algorithmic Marketing at Sell Side*. While we are on the topic of investment, we continue the topic through to the last two coding chapters—Chapter 8, *Building Personal Wealth Advisers with Bank APIs* and Chapter 9, *Mass Customization of Client Lifetime Wealth*—by zooming in on the wealth management perspective.

The final chapter helps us to focus on the data aggregation issue at the client end. Essentially, all of the bank's clients – individuals, corporations, and institutions—will own and manage their data in a centralized manner in order to cultivate their own asset—data.

Consumer markets help us to see the various types of components that are designed to push the frontier of data management. While in the case of institutions and corporations, the data pertaining to the legal entity is significantly more complex, a better knowledge management model is required to organize the depth of data describing the corporations.

In fact, the manner in which we organize business- and institution-related data is a topic that is no longer discussed in the era of knowledge management, even though it was once a thriving subject in business schools in the early 2000s.

Models and frameworks were proposed in the sphere of knowledge management, but the technological solutions designed to harvest this knowledge with minimal effort are lacking on the part of many organizations. Working in a consulting firm back then, I witnessed the pain of maintaining the body of knowledge, which is the core asset of the consulting industry—business know-how. Now, we will return to this topic as we are going to make our machine smart and make financial decisions at an expert level. The boundaries of robots will be expanded when we can explicitly maintain them in the name of data quality management.

Implications for banking professionals

Never-ending debates are taking place regarding the changes in business models currently used by banks. My personal view is that the core decisions regarding forward-looking risk and return forecasts remain. Ultimately, we need a bank to fund future activity that is not completely certain at the time a financial decision is made. We are also making a decision regarding our future wealth, which we also do not have full control of. What has changed is the speed of update of this risk and return view as a result of machines and the rapid increase in the number of these expert decisions being left to laypeople.

Looking at the banking industry today, it is not just banking professionals, but also governments, regulators, and consumers who will push the boundaries together to create more efficient financial markets, with a free flow of data with clear ownership and technologies to attribute the values provided by the data in all walks of decision making.

Across industry, Open API remains a pain point for incumbents, while it is a topic where new entrants are crying foul, according to Michel E. Porter's *Five Forces*, in terms of the competitive positioning of companies.

Alongside the open bank API, which is just a gateway to get data, no worthwhile discussion is taking place on banking data standards for customers and clients. Indeed, APIs appear fashionable, but they also pose a huge problem in terms of dealing with how data is stored by customers for their own benefit. It seems less than ideal for individual customers to consider this topic, since the usability of the data will be polarized between those who can organize and those who cannot.

Implications for regulators

Gone are the days when instructions to banks were *best-effort*; models and validation are now in place to guarantee the quality of services and to protect investors' interests. Investors need to know the features that can create volatility in financial valuations. Perhaps timeliness becomes a key instead of expecting banks to have definite views about what might happen? The probability regarding risky events set by banks can be validated.

Implications for government

How do we provide a technology to allow individuals to own their data? How is the government taking the lead when it comes to storing an individual's identity as well as all their footprints? Personal data standards would help to reduce the economics of sharing, storing, and having individuals manage their own data.

GDPR in Europe is a good regulation, but it essentially lacks the technology required to execute it, as in the case of knowledge management. Likewise, data that describes interactions between companies, corporations, institutions, and public markets will be considered utilities provided by the government, as stock exchanges own the data.

Following the philosophy of public benefit, the objective is not to make huge profit but to provide public services that facilitate other economic activities. I believe more government intervention is warranted with regard to how public domain data is distributed. This will give robots an easier environment in which to work as the data availability issue underpins the entire book. It is not hard to see how it creates a bigger drag on AI adoption in all walks of economic activity. Counterbalancing this openness in relation to data, again, we require better control of the data—for companies and individuals alike.

The open data movement has been a buzzword in terms of allowing data to be available. Open government data may touch on issues such as stock exchange data, which is sometimes run by quasi-government organizations under specific licenses or regulations. Likewise, open bank data is also driven by global financial regulators as a driving force to provide bank customers with their own data.

At a practical level, data is a key ingredient for AI, and in some cases, it is cleansed, maintained, and provided as a benefit that costs taxpayers money! However, the resources spent on data maintenance also depend on the AI use cases that generate cost savings in terms of automated and better decision making. By this simple logic, someone has to pay: either through a shared pool in the government budget (that is, taxpayers, including you) or those who use the data (you again!). And one of the challenges in terms of data being accessible is to track its usage. It is considerably easier if we want to ask anyone who has used the data to pay on the particular data point down to the field level.

AI can be the electricity of tomorrow, but data will first be provided as the electricity of today.

How to come up with features and acquire the domain knowledge

In all the chapters so far, we have not explained where we get this domain knowledge from. A typical AI project requires us to slip into the shoes of finance professionals. Where to begin? The following is a list that will help you:

- **Textbook and training courses**: The easiest path to follow is to follow how these professionals are trained. These courses contain the jargon, methodologies, and processes designed for the respective work type.
- **Research papers in banking and finance**: When it comes to finding the right data, research in finance and banking can prove to be a very valuable resource. It will not only show where to get the data; it will also showcase those features with strong powers of prediction. However, I normally do not get lost in the inconsistency of features across authors and markets. I simply include them all as far as possible—with the support of theory by researchers.
- **Observing the dashboards**: BI captures the key features that are meaningful to human users. The data fields used in those BI reports are good features that can vividly describe the problems as stipulated by human experts.
- **Procedural manuals**: In case you are working in an established organization with processes and procedures in place, it serves as a valuable source to describe how humans work, especially those processing intensive works.
- **Institutions**: Some say design thinking, some say it is just putting yourself into the shoes of others, by trying to work on the task in a hypothetical manner.

- **Observing child development**: In case it is related to tasks such as perceiving and communicating information, we can observe how humans learn to build up the components and understand what a neural architecture should look like.
- **Looking for Excel**: Excel has become a dominant tool in business schools, and is a semi-standardized form of decision making, especially in the area of financial modeling. This serves as a good starting point to understand how humans make decisions and the complex rules associated with doing so.

The preceding points cover business domain considerations, but we also need to consider the IT aspect of rolling out the model.

IT production considerations in connection with AI deployment

AI is just a file if the algorithm is not run in the day-to-day decision making of banks. The trend, of course, is to provide AI as a service to the software developers who write the program. This aside, there are a list of items that require the following:

- **Encryption**: Data is key and all the AI runs on sensitive data. Even though the data is anonymized somewhat with the scalers that change the data into the range of zero to one. Encryption remains important, however, in making sure that the encryption is in place when the data is in transit via the network and remains with an encrypted database.
- **Load balancing**: Handling requests with the correct capacity to handle, as well as creating sufficient servers to run the algorithm, are required. With the trend of going serverless with a cloud provider, the issue appears to have abated somewhat. However, the issue still remains; it is just being outsourced. Being an engineer, having an appreciation of capacity and how to handle loading is about the level of service. We want a smart robot that is always available, instead of having a smart engine that disappears when people are in desperate need. To do so requires an appreciation of usage traffic, hardware and software capacity planning, as well as a means to execute it alongside the traffic change.
- **Authentication**: Organizations normally have their own preferences for regarding authentication. It can have quite an impact on customer experiences while security remains a concern.

Where to look for more use cases

AI applications listed in this book largely focus on front-office banking services; the back-office processing jobs are not covered in any great detail. Stepping back, where should you look out for opportunities in case you wish to start your own project?

- **Long hours; boring job**: Boring means repetitive, and that's where machines thrive and data is rich.
- **Large labor force**: When it comes to business cases, it is easy to look for jobs that have high levels of employment. This means a huge business potential and easy-to-justify implementation. This constitutes a huge challenge for HR professionals.
- **High pay**: If we were to make finance accessible, can we make these highly paid jobs even more productive? In the case of investment bankers, security structurers, and hedge fund traders, how can their non-productive time be reduced?
- **Unique dataset**: If the dataset is not accessible to outsiders, the chance of the domain not being looked at is high since researchers and start-ups cannot detect this problem.

Which areas require more practical research?

In certain areas, this book has hit the ceiling of research, and these are the research areas that could help move AI applications in banking:

- **Autonomous learning**: AI will be replacing the works of AI engineers—given that the machine will be able to learn. Given the wealth of data nowadays, the machine will adopt its network structure itself.
- **Transparent AI**: As the machine starts to make decisions, humans will demand transparency as regards the decision-making process.
- **Body of knowledge**: In the case of expert knowledge, further research will look at how organizations can use AI to generate the body of knowledge. Practically, the Wikipedia form stored in BERT or any language model is not intended for human consumption or knowledge cultivation. And how do we squeeze the knowledge map to form a neural network, and vice versa?

- **Data masking**: To allow data to travel and exchange freely, a flexible data-masking mechanism that preserves distribution characteristics within a field and in between data fields is important. It allows data to be shared with researchers or even open sourced for attack by smart data scientists. A secondary question in connection with a good masking mechanism is whether data owners can share their data with research communities in order to work on real-world challenges? Is this regarded as a donation and is therefore tax deductible?

- **Data aggregation and standardization**: As covered earlier in this chapter, this describes how client data is standardized and how individuals and companies are allowed to own and manage their data.

- **Cross-disciplinary task focus applications**: To uncover more research topics, it is very important for researchers from different disciplines to work together in solving a task focus problem, rather than working on dataset that is meant to tackle a single research topic.

- **Data life cycle technologies**: Since data is used in so many places, and is altered, updated, and copied across systems, do we have the right technology to keep track of all of these movements? Once we can track its movement, we can then attribute the values to the contributors of data in the supply chain to incentivize data production. Some advocate blockchain, but saving huge amounts of data on blockchain does not seem practical.

Summary

This book is designed to illustrate the current possibilities in terms of technology using public domain information. I hope that it helps to create a supply of talent and researchers to aid the industry. It also creates a base level of performance that any potential start-up needs to beat in order to be qualified. With all code in books now being open source, I am happy to be at the bottom of performance with regard to technological solutions!

There are too many books that are purely visionary, and there are also books that talk about the technical considerations without getting to the heart of the problem. There are books full of mathematics and formulas that deal with encrypted knowledge. This book is here to bridge the gap between the vision and the technical considerations. I believe that future generations deserve to study in an AI utopia before they come to change our world of work. For professionals in the industry and those wishing to upgrade their skills, I hope that this book can suggest a number of areas of interest to consolidate further.

This is just the beginning.

Other Books You May Enjoy

If you enjoyed this book, you may be interested in these other books by Packt:

Artificial Intelligence By Example - Second Edition
Denis Rothman

ISBN: 978-1-83921-153-9

- Apply k-nearest neighbors (KNN) to language translations and explore the opportunities in Google Translate
- Understand chained algorithms combining unsupervised learning with decision trees
- Solve the XOR problem with feedforward neural networks (FNN) and build its architecture to represent a data flow graph
- Learn about meta learning models with hybrid neural networks
- Create a chatbot and optimize its emotional intelligence deficiencies with tools such as Small Talk and data logging
- Building conversational user interfaces (CUI) for chatbots
- Writing genetic algorithms that optimize deep learning neural networks
- Build quantum computing circuits

PyTorch Artificial Intelligence Fundamentals
Jibin Mathew

ISBN: 978-1-83855-704-1

- Perform tensor manipulation using PyTorch
- Train a fully connected neural network
- Advance from simple neural networks to convolutional neural networks (CNNs) and recurrent neural networks (RNNs)
- Implement transfer learning techniques to classify medical images
- Get to grips with generative adversarial networks (GANs), along with their implementation
- Build deep reinforcement learning applications and learn how agents interact in the real environment
- Scale models to production using ONNX Runtime
- Deploy AI models and perform distributed training on large datasets

Leave a review - let other readers know what you think

Please share your thoughts on this book with others by leaving a review on the site that you bought it from. If you purchased the book from Amazon, please leave us an honest review on this book's Amazon page. This is vital so that other potential readers can see and use your unbiased opinion to make purchasing decisions, we can understand what our customers think about our products, and our authors can see your feedback on the title that they have worked with Packt to create. It will only take a few minutes of your time, but is valuable to other potential customers, our authors, and Packt. Thank you!

Index

Z

Zillow
URL 186

www.ingramcontent.com/pod-product-compliance
Lightning Source LLC
Chambersburg PA
CBHW060111090326
40690CB00064B/4987